# DIVINE ORDER OF AUTHORITY, Law and Mathematics

*There is always a line of divine order in every fibre of His creation and no one has the right to violate it.*

## A Call to Conscience

Maxwell V. Blackwood

10-10-10 Publishing

DIVINE ORDER OF AUTHORITY, Law and Mathematics
www.divineorderbook.com


Paperback ISBN: 978-1-77277-457-3

Second edition March 2022



Publisher
10-10-10 Publishing
Markham, ON
Canada

Printed in Canada and the United States of America

**DIVINE ORDER**
**OF**
**AUTHORITY**
**Law and Mathematics**

Now available, the book for the 21th century and beyond, by popular demand and long awaited; *Divine Order of Authority, Law and Mathematics.* This book is a must for your library. Get your personal copy, for family and friends.
Available at Amazon and our office at:

1944 Eglinton Ave. West, Toronto, ON. Canada. M6E 2J8

Direct line: 647-550-5739     Office: 647-348-0606

doalm@divineorderbook.com
www.divineorderbook.com

# TABLE OF CONTENTS

# List of Appendices

*There is always a line of divine order in every fibre of His creation, and no one has the right to violate it.*
A Call to Conscience

# Foreword

**Written from the heart and should be read by the heart.**

*Divine Order of Authority* is unique and timely in more ways than one. It does not need a commercial promotion. This book is written from that special location in life where the creator and man meet by the unifying power of love. It is written from the heart and should be read by the heart. By that we mean both the intellect and nobility of intention.

Like all good writers that history has known, Maxwell works from the pyramid of humility and love. When that is compounded with his vast experience, ethical pastoral work, a lifetime of encouraging others, and avid volunteerism, then you have a work like this, a diamond piece that does not come our way very often. I commend you to learn from this book and share it with others; for love, for empowerment, for a better life, for a future that we can march to in confidence, unity, and vigour.

**Professor Salah J. Hussein**

## Philippians 4:8

"Finally, brethren, whatsoever things are true, whatsoever things are honest, whatsoever things are just, whatsoever things are pure, whatsoever things are lovely, whatsoever things are of good report; if there be any virtue,
and if there be any praise, think on these things."

King James Version (KJV)

*It is a time honoured, popular wisdom, that a book will find its reader. It is our ardent hope that this happens here and now and this book finds its readers.*

## Words for Thought

*Upon falling down under the cutting force of the axe, a tree screamed: O axe, you could not have cut me down if you didn't have part of me in you.*

*– Samali saying*

*Of All The Things I Have Lost, I Miss My Mind The Most.*

This book is presented to:

From:

Message:

# Dedication

This book is in honour of my illustrious patriots, my parents Theodore Blackwood (affectionately called Teaman) and my beloved mother, Evelyn Blackwood. It is also dedicated to my three children—Andrew Blackwood (my first born), Valrie Blackwood (my daughter) and David Blackwood (affectionately called King David)—and Prince Damias Blackwood (grandson), my wife Norma Lewis-Blackwood and, by extension, the Blackwood family, and friends around the world. Even though I never met my mother, as she died when I was a baby, I learned that she complimented my father for being kind and supportive, like a good wife and matriarch should.

I am highlighting my father in particular, who was not only the best father, patriarch and friend but a multi-genius like Imhotep of Egypt, the father of medicine, and an architect, a mathematician, a preacher, a teacher, a land surveyor and a community developer, who was also highly respected. I always make reference to my father. He reminds me of the great nobleman, Job, in the holy book. It is written and remains written in the holy scripture of Job, that when he would pass by the wayside, people would stop misbehaving and even put their hands over their mouths in respect. Growing up with my dad, as a little boy in Jamaica, I saw the same expressions from the people. Just to give an insight of my father for those who did not know him, he was well respected, and I think this happened because he respected everyone, even persons classified as objectionable and the marginalized.

I have many nieces and nephews who are all special to me; however, I am highlighting, specifically, my nephew Desmond Davis, who plays a significant role in my business and manages my finances. He is easier to talk to when compared to many others about various subjects.

Special tribute to my brother-in-law Noel Johnson, who taught me and many other youth the vocational art of jewelry and watch making.

I hereby pay tribute and remembrance to my brothers and sisters, the living as well as the ones who have passed on: Willis Blackwood, Lester Blackwood, Alti Blackwood, Roy Blackwood, Kenneth Blackwood, Fred Blackwood, Arvil Blackwood, Minette Blackwood-Robinson, Edna Blackwood-Boyne, Sylvia Blackwood, Dolsey Blackwood-Slater, Thelma Blackwood-Elphick, Rudel Blackwood, Daphne Una-Lee Blackwood-Bygrave, Cherry Blackwood-Lewis (twin), Ethlyn Blackwood-Rankin (twin), Lurline Anderson-Blackwood, Estrie Foster-Blackwood.

# Acknowledgements

**Special acknowledgement, praise and worship to our Creator, The Sovereign (Eternal), for His boundless, unbounding love and mercies. For His mercies endureth forever.**

Professor Salah Jama Hussein, who made his contribution by assisting with two articles for the appendix in this book, and assisting with the editing.

My office assistant/graphic designer, Shamar Brown-Smith, who is dedicated, focused and reliable from the start of his employment in my business.

My niece and assistant editor, Julia Montieth, who has been a team player and very reliable throughout the years.

# Preface

This book, *The Divine Order of Authority,* is designed to define what constitutes law. While it is imperative to define the law, it is important, to the highest degree, to understand or comprehend what is the purpose of the law. Law and mathematics are the constitutions that govern and operate the universe as designed by the Creator (Yahweh). Laws are designed by the Creator for order and harmony, and for us as humans to have a happy life. Therefore, we can say that the laws are the transcript of God's character. In other words, He lives by these principles.

There are different types of laws in the universe. There are many misunderstandings by millions of people about these laws, and they even go as far as saying that these laws of the Ten Commandments are nailed to the cross, but it is imperative to make the distinction of which laws we are talking about. One should always bear in mind that there are many laws in nature. In most cases, people ignorantly make reference to the laws of the Ten Commandments as nailed to the cross, but that was never the case.

In the universe, there are many types of laws, and none of them were nailed to the cross. All laws have their place in the universe, such as the law of nature (natural law), law of health, law of gravity, decomposition and anthropy, to name a few. If there is an iota or any shift in, for example, the laws of gravity, we would be essentially floating in space.

What to understand innately is that the Eternal, the Sovereign One, governs the universe through His laws; most of all including the moral Ten Commandments as in the book of Exodus 20. The old rascal, the adversarial one called the devil, tricks people, and the people trick themselves into believing that those laws were nailed to the cross. Anyone who believes these things deceives himself. The law is designed not to restrict us, as has been taught by some foolish people, but is designed to bring total happiness and bliss.

These laws have teeth; you break them, they break you. Like the law of health, if you drink poison, you know the consequences of that because these are living laws. Anyone who teaches—and I mean anyone—that these laws are not relevant and are done away with, damnation to that group or one who teaches that. Again, for emphasis, laws are designed to protect us in certain boundaries for our own good.

Another word for law is order (order means law); hence, you get the title in the Canadian television series *Law and Order*. If you don't have order, you have chaos, and chaos is what we have today on planet Earth because people reject the "thus saith the Lord" and His holy ordinances, the law. A great many persons are going around and deceiving the people by speaking out from both sides of their mouths (lying). Beware of them!

Remember, law and order are somewhat similar and, where order is lacking, there is disarray. You should also bear in mind that not everything should have a contrast to make sense. With that said, it would be madness to suggest that law can be done away with. Finally, there is a connection between darkness and light, which many of us do not realize. The forces that produce darkness also produce light, and they are basically a filter of each other. When darkness or shadow recedes, the light takes its prominence, and vice versa, meaning when light recedes, darkness also takes its pre-eminence.

# Introduction

Whenever I discuss a subject matter that is secular or sacred, it is very important—most important—to address the issue and view the subject matter from the correct prism, the beginning, proper context and from a cause and effect perspective. Although this book is not a spiritual manual, I will attempt to address most if not all the issues that concern us as humans, from a spiritual perspective. All our concerns as humans always have a duality: spiritual and physical. Everything that I pen will reflect those two dimensions in life.

One of the root causes of the problems in our world today is that people seem to lack or are unable to apprehend the correct knowledge and concept of the true purpose in life. Some of the deepest concerns of the human heart are questions such as these:

- Why did life originate?
- What constitutes the heart of the universe?
- Who are we?
- Why do bad things happen to good people?

No physical or chemical data can explain these legitimate questions as they are spiritual in nature and need the correct spiritual response.

I would like to make myself abundantly clear. This book is not scholarly or academic, notwithstanding that most of the subject matters I will be discussing in this book are being discussed at the moment by the intelligent, and attempts have been made to explain by the philosophers. It is important to note then, when matters of importance are discussed by humans whose intelligence is limited at best, in man's explanation there is no finality. In apprehending this fact, I am always ready to share ideas and discuss any subject based on its merit, and this is why I am compelled to write this book.

*Throughout this book, I will endeavour to speak from the correct frame of reference.*

# The Purpose of Law and Mathematics as a Divine Constitution

I personally believe that all of us humans have different grades of intelligence by nature. Therefore, our nervous system is set up differently. We all have different dominant attributes, and each one of us has something to share with the others in the world. If we do not give this special gift to the world and the people of the world, and we die with that special gift, we would have cheated the people, ourselves, our Creator and our brothers and sisters. It could be a small poem or a painting. The gift of caring is one of the basic privileges we could share. Whatever you are blessed with, share it. Do not cheat the world by dying with your gift, but always share it while you are alive.

It has been said that most of the knowledge and wisdom is at the graveyard, and the reason is that people did not care to share what they know. They fail to apprehend that any gifts they are given from the most merciful One, be it wealth or knowledge, must be shared. It has been said that the only thing we keep is what we give away, and I know how strange this concept may sound to some people in a world of so much individualism, greed and ego. Remember what we said before, that when the student is ready, the teacher will appear. If you just take a moment and observe nature, it will teach you a thing or two in that score. One of the first lessons from nature is that it is always giving and sharing from itself; that is the nature of life. If you want to live an abundant life, start by sharing today; and by giving and sharing, that is when you start living. One of the best ways to share is "Isness." Just be your natural self; it could just be a smile you have to give. Do you know how much a smile is worth? Not a million dollars. In fact, it is priceless.

Whenever you give something away, do not think for a moment that you lose a thing. The truth is that both the giver and receiver acquire a blessing, and the blessings are in the act itself. It remains written in the holy volume that it is better to give away the self, and that is also designed as a divine order to starve self and the ego. To receive is easy, but to give cheerfully, you have to be balanced. That is, you know the order of things and the nature of things. When you think giving is living, every day you must look out for opportunities to help, not just wait to be asked.

Again, if we observe the wonder of nature around us, every facet in the universe gives to each other—the rivers flow to the sea, and the sun's warmth gives life to our planet in abundance. Nature always gives in abundance, unlike mankind. Remember, whatever measure you give, you will receive. If you give much, you will receive much, and if you give little, you will receive little. Whatever you receive is commensurate with your efforts.

Any person who chooses to know the Eternal, spiritually speaking, needs to know the order of the Eternal. The title of this book is *Divine Order of Authority*, and there is a reason why I have chosen this title. This reason is due to my observation through my studies that the Eternal has set up a specific order and protocol, a rule of engagement and arrangement if you please, in every aspect of His creation. One of the reasons I think the Eternal, in His boundless favour, set up this divine order, is because He wants us to receive an abundant and fulfilling life. If we as individuals or as nations neglect the divine order, we will not experience this true fulfillment in our lives. This lack in human nature is a direct reason for the greed and violence we are experiencing in our society today. It will only get worse if we continue to neglect the divine order.

Remember, order means law, and just like the television show, *Law and Order*, law is designed to give balance, and we are not just talking about moral law. There are laws in every aspect of God's creation, and the Eternal made use of His immutable law to carry out His will so that order and balance can be maintained in the universe. There are some popular beliefs going around that the immutable laws of the Eternal do not apply today, and that supposition is what I call the highest form of insanity. Do you really know what you are talking about, and do you have any concept or knowledge about why the Eternal Most Holy designed His divine law? They are for our own good, and whenever you or I decide through free choice to reject the Eternal or His law, do you know what you are rejecting? Think for a moment about that.

Let us think for a moment also about one of God's laws, the law of gravity. Let us suppose in a flash of a moment that the law dissipates—are you aware of the chaos and violence that it will cause to this planet? Our little Earth would be hurled out of space, and what would happen to all of us beggarly little people on planet Earth? Are you realizing the importance of divine law? And please remember that man cannot make law, only God can. Man can only make rules and regulations that change with time, while God's laws are timeless and immutable and unchangeable.

I have talked with many people, and my observation is that the law that they talk about, the law that they claim is not applied, is the law of the Ten Commandments, which are the moral laws. As important as the law of gravity is, the moral law of the Ten Commandments supersedes any other law; the moral law deals with your thoughts and emotions. It is at the centre of your being. If the moral laws were changeable, the Christ—the real historic Jesus of Nazareth—would not have to enter this world on the all-important rescue mission. He did come to save all of mankind. That verified moral law is unchangeable and timeless, and we are the ones who need to be changed today, not the holy divine law. As we have said before, and it also remains written, the law is the transcript of the most holy eternal character, timeless glory, and I rest my case.

Let the Eternal remain true and all men be liars. There are protocols and rules of engagement, or order, in our physical, everyday lives. For example, if you get in your car to go to work, you will not reach work if you just open the car door and just sit there. That is a rule of engagement, and in order to follow, you have to start the car, put it in gear, put your seat belt on for our own security and drive on. Divine order is even more important, and all laws, moral or natural, are for our good, peace and happiness. We cannot overemphasize the importance of divine order.

The universe operates on law, which is order, and the Eternal makes use of His divine law as a medium, to carry out His divine will for our own good so that we can have balance. Balance produces harmony, which is the opposite of chaos. Can you even imagine the chaos that this planet would be going through if the laws of physics, gravity and chemistry became tilted out of balance or even rendered non-existent. If these laws of nature just make a little shift and are tilted out of balance (even rendered nonexistent) from their natural path as they were designed by the good Lord, the harm and ensuing destruction is incalculable. This Earth would be thrust into chaos. It is important to note also that the laws of God do not discriminate, and if you break them, they will break you.

From the king or the queen to the pope or to the ordinary soul, we are all equal before the law, and we hear this repeated all the time in this corrupt world. The citizenry see the opposite; they see the rich and the powerful literally get away with murder. And it may enter your mind to think and say to yourself, "Why bother to do the right thing when I see the wicked just prospering. The rich and the powerful keep getting away with murder." It seems like this to those who are on the verge of giving up because it does not make sense to do the right thing.

I say to you to pause a moment and back up and think. Many things and different products will not make any sense to our senses. One thing is left when everything is sinking, and that is the living and written Word, which you can trust. It remains written in the holy volume that the Eternal, the most merciful, will never ever forget the good we do, however small; and while everyone will forget, the good Lord will not. With this in mind, take heart and cheer up. This is where we get the concept of law and order. If we do not obey the stipulated laws, and if we do not have proper law and order in the home, we will have kids suffer and die. Moreover, we will have chaos in the home without laws, and we will produce a dysfunctional family and a dysfunctional society.

Let this point be emphasized that law, which if respected, will produce peace and happiness. The law was designed for our good.

## Establishing Who You Are

As human beings, to have proper respect for divine order, we first of all have to establish who we are and what we are composed of. We have to have some kind of self-knowledge of ourselves. Have you ever wondered what it means to be a human being? Once we are in the mode of some kind of self-examination, we will quickly start asking some even more important questions, like "who am I," "where did I come from" and most importantly, "where do I/we go from here?" These questions are actually spiritual in nature, and once you have a handle on that, the next quest is to start the journey to get to have some knowledge or concept of who the Eternal really is.

Once a person has some knowledge of themselves and of their nature, and of who the Eternal is, only then will His divine order be allowed or given respect. Furthermore, for the first time, we will take pleasure in following these divine orders that the Eternal most gracious designed for our good pleasure or happiness.

Now that we have established the importance of order (protocol and divine order) in practicing, and their role in our lives, we can go from here to discuss some of these all important divine orders of authority.

## The Eternal Is Unknowable

Whenever I am given the opportunity to speak on behalf of the Eternal God, I always like to use the word "Eternal" for the English word "God," and "Yeshua" for the English word "Jesus." Proper usage of the words gives proper frequency and importance. I am aware that no human language can describe the Eternal, so I chose the language that describes a better concept or ideas, and that is all human languages can do to give the human concept of the Eternal.

Who is unknowable and unnamable from a spiritually metaphorical point of view? The Eternal is the only reality in the universe. All other creations, regardless of their rank or grade by creation, have a beginning, and hold or owe their existence (GLORY!!!) to the Eternal alone.

The languages I prefer to use when trying to use human concepts to talk about the Eternal One, are Hebrew, Aramaic and a little Greek. These languages are more original and give a better or more comprehensive concept than the English language, which does not make a distinction between ideas and things. In other words, there is an element of sharpness and exactitude in the spiritual orientation of the Aramaic and Hebrew languages, as compared to the dry, commerce-oriented, violent, imperial language of the English language. Whatever human concept or ideas we have of the Eternal, we have to realize it does not necessarily mean that is how the Eternal is in reality. Infinite times, it has been said that the Eternal has not chosen to reveal His name at this time, but will do so at the time of His choosing, and we do not have to worry about that at the present moment.

## The Eternal Is Sovereign

One of the first divine orders of authority is that the Eternal (God) alone is sovereign over all, and His orders and instructions are final. The Eternal and the Eternal alone have the right to change His divine principles; no human can or has the right to alter even a dot. As I have said earlier in our discussion, once we know who we are, and who the Eternal is or will ever be, we will be encouraged to govern our lives according to His divine order, and will experience a great transformation. There will be a change in our lives for the betterment of the whole family.

The Eternal's (God) name is unutterable, and no human can call or pronounce the Eternal's name at this time; He will choose a time and place to reveal His name. Again, we do not have to worry at this moment about that at this moment.

We can only worship the Eternal through His name, so the great noble men and women of the holy book chose names, and names that were chosen by himself, the Eternal, to address His person (himself). One of the best ways to realize the Eternal is as a personal friend who came to love you, which does not mean for a moment that the Eternal is a person like us or anything we know. I am just using a human concept to suggest that one of the best ways to realize the Eternal should be like a personal friend. The Eternal (God) has many names, such as Yahweh, El Shaddai or Adonai. All these names are given to address Him, and all the Eternal names are holy and must be treated with much reverence. These names are holy because they are used to ascribe worship to the Eternal alone, but it does not mean that these names are the real names of the Eternal.

To name one is very important in biblical and historical times. Names are not just to identify, as is the case in the Western cultures. Names actually describe a person's spiritual grade or even land of origin; so much so that upon calling a person, or evoking their memory, we are engaged in an activity higher than our calling—we are inviting to life again.

## What's in a Name?

The Eternal's name in Biblical times was held in the highest honour and reverence. Other names were employed and used to address the Lord. These names that are extended to address the Eternal were taken from the holy Word and emit very positive energy. So our ancestors did not use these names carelessly like our present day generation. Our children and ourselves as adults are at risk if we continue to show contempt for the most holy name of the Eternal in our places of worship. Remember, we worship the Eternal through His name.

For all to receive the highest blessing from the Eternal name, we need to choose the correct name. It has been said in the holy book that the Eternal will come from different ways and bless all who call Him by His right name. The Eternal's name is powerful (full of power).

Although the sun shines on the good and the evil, The Eternal does not show partiality; and He, the Eternal, transcends worship and songs. In the same breath, He always honours or blesses those who express reverence for His most holy name. In the Lord's Prayer, Yeshua teaches His hearers to hallow the Lord's name.

## Worshipping the Eternal Only

Now that we have a more informed concept of the Eternal name, we should have a desire to worship Him in that manner. If you notice carefully, I use the expression "Him"; however, by now we should know that the Eternal transcends gender, so the expression is just a human concept. The Eternal is a spirit and is neither male nor female. We can worship the Eternal only with our minds and through His most holy name, and although the Eternal has many names to describe different aspects of His attributes, we know that this vast world or the vast universe is created by the Eternal God.

One of the Eternal's most gracious divine orders is that he does not tolerate rivalry. "Here O Israel your Lord" (the Eternal Lord is one). Millions of stars are placed in the skies by one God, the Eternal. The idea that because we humans have a desire to worship the Eternal, and that we came just to go ahead and worship, is not entirely true. Although the Eternal takes pleasure when we worship Him in spirit and in truth, in truth and in fact, we should realize that we humans have to ask for permission to first enter His presence in prayer, and the Eternal has to give us permission to worship Him.

Notwithstanding that Yeshua the Christ encourages us to come to His throne with boldness or with confidence, that statement does not imply that we should just barge into the presence of the Eternal without proper protocol. This whole book is about following proper protocol so that we can receive the best result in every facet of our lives, spiritual and secular.

The Eternal alone is sovereign and, therefore, has the right to be worshipped, meaning all creation worships the Eternal with delight. We humans generally think we are the only ones who worship, and that human languages are the only or best way to communicate. In fact, there are many other self-expressions that transcend languages, and they all give glory and praise to the most gracious.

The Psalms stated that there is no language or sound, yet their voices are heard. We humans think that we are doing the Eternal a favour when we worship (Him). What ignorance and arrogance. As we discuss the Eternal out of His highest favour, given the privileges and permission to worship, we cannot just worship the Eternal because we feel like doing so. Those who choose to worship the Eternal out of sublime amour by the Eternal's most gracious permission, will worship with spirit and in truth. We need to know, first of all, that the Eternal has no lack whatsoever.

On the subject of worship, if we were taught that we as humans were created to worship the most gracious One, and if we do not have a proper appreciation of what that means, then with the lack of knowledge in our nature as humans, we may be tempted to think that we are doing the Eternal a favour when we worship Him or when we do something good. It is true that all creation, including man, who are given this awesome brain to think and choose, must use this brain to worship, and that worship should be at each breath we take at each moment.

When we praise and think of the Eternal's boundless mercies and favours to us, I am shown that is not enough to ask. All of the Eternal God's creations can't wait to praise; man is the only one debating whether or not it's the right thing to do. Worship benefits us humans, not the Eternal. Remember, the Eternal has no lack whatsoever, but we humans are the ones with the lack or need. Humans are the ones with greed, and are full of violence and need to be saved from themselves.

The next time we think of worshipping the Eternal, let us pause for a moment and meditate. Meditation is very important because it helps to remove the limitation of languages and theories, so that one's mind will be in a correct state once they are in the right frame of mind. We will quickly realize that we are very privileged to be given permission based on our free will, to choose to worship the most gracious Eternal. ***Praise be He and exalted be His fame forever.***

Worship celebrates our needs and puts us in touch with substantive reality. We must always know that we are privileged to be given the permission to worship and praise the Eternal. As humans, we are the ones who are called to take part in the eternal bounties, which are unbounded. ***Praise be He.*** Let us think for a moment as ordinary people, notwithstanding that ordinary people and ordinary things are the most profound, like the smile or cry of a baby. What I am trying to say is that not one of us ordinary individuals can fly to Jordan and just barge into the king's earthly human chambers without any invitation and permission to see the king. It is much more so when we come in the presence of the King of all kings, the most holy sublime One. We as humans must come with bent minds and knees (by mind first), with much reverence and godly fear in the name of Yeshua the Christ, with permission. With permission, we will be made whole.

# There Are Different Beginnings and, in Some Dimensions, There Are No Beginnings

In the beginning (prehistoric times), the Eternal created all things beautiful in His own time. It is important that we apprehend at this moment that there are several beginnings. The beginning, we will realize, is the creation of this planet. You have the beginning of beginnings. As far as the most Holy One is concerned, He transcends time, space and matter. Time begins with man, and the Eternal has no beginning. Our three dimensional mind is not calibrated to decipher such concepts.

As was mentioned before, substantiated reality like the Eternal (***blessed be He)*** is not knowable or nameable. Whatever we apprehend about the Eternal, even the most fertile mind is based on human concept and cannot describe fully, in any way, what the Eternal is. Those of us who are looking for or to the Eternal to prove His existence to us, will receive no proof except our own temporary existence that is given to us by His most gracious favour, to develop character so that we can receive real life abundance in and through the gracious favour of Yeshua the Christ.

## The Origin of Disobedience and Rebellion

Our loving, most gracious Lord makes all things most beautiful and bright at creation, for the benefit of all humanity. The big question is, where did all the crime, violence and injustice come from? It is of great importance that we apprehend the nature of the Eternal. It is safe to say, based on all of creation, the very nature of the Eternal is honour, notwithstanding that one of His divine orders is that He decreed that man must choose. As humans, we are given the choice to obey or disobey our maker. Not only humans were given this gift, but the angelic host (angels), regardless of their rank, also had to choose to obey or disobey.

Someone expressed the view that when the Eternal gives humans the ability to make a choice freely, it is a big risk the Eternal is taking. This is just a human concept of the Eternal, and I am not sure that it is right; as a human myself, I do not enjoy receiving anything from another person unless it was given to me freely by choice. *I think the good Lord respects our decision, good or bad, once it is made from free choice.* The Eternal goes out of His way, humanly speaking, to inform us of the consequences of our decision, good or bad. I think it is time to stop blaming the Eternal most gracious for the wrong choices we make, and to start taking responsibility, because the Eternal is most merciful and full of mercy, if we are serious about changing to do His will that is good for us. He will save us even at this moment.

As a human, I must stand up to defend the most gracious, not that He needs my help. I am the beggar, frail in understanding, and stand hopelessly in need of His mercies. Furthermore, I have to say something to the effect of making a personal decision, that I am tired of myself and other humans blaming the good Lord for the problems we bring on ourselves. What we need to do is just repent and ask for His mercies and accept responsibility for our actions.

There was a time when this universe beat as one harmony everywhere (as we would say), and I will say it again that the Eternal most gracious makes all things beautiful. There is no easy language to express how rebellion got started in the distant past. There was one of the Eternal creations from the angelic order that chose to rebel. There are different ranks of angels, and the idea that everything was created equal is false. In fact, even two leaves on the same tree are not the same. In regard to the angel who was called Lucifer, the one who brings light, the expression was made in the holy book that the misturning of evil was found in the angel. Let's be clear; the Eternal Most Holy did not create a devil, or Satan. The angel Lucifer made a devil out of himself. In just the same way, when we as humans choose to reject the divine order that is designed to bring us peace and happiness, we all make fools of ourselves. *Stop blaming the most merciful One!!*

What is causing the greed and violence in the world today is our ego. It has been said that once we find a self, the possibilities always exist that we humans want to exalt that self above others, and that is a part of the root cause of greed and justice—the self or ego. We have said early in our discussion that for anyone to have a proper appreciation of any problem, they have to look at the issue from a cause and effect perspective, as it never fails. The end is in the beginning, and so is the beginning in the end. The cause is in the effect, so the effect is in the cause. These questions are not simple, and I am not trying to explain them, but I am just sharing ideas and concepts as I apprehend them. Each of us has to do our own research and studies. My humble advice is, whenever you read, or view the television or listen to the radio, always think for yourself and be your own editor.

## The Ego and Selfishness

Now that we have arrived at some appreciation of why individuals and nations are experiencing the kind of chaos, violence and injustice that is in our world, we conclude that the real cause is our ego, which will in turn cause us to rebel against our Creator. Once self is in the picture, we convince ourselves that we cannot trust anyone; we will not even trust our ego, even to the Almighty, the most merciful. That is how self-deception is serious and dangerous.

The Eternal created a master plan to save us from ourselves. This rescue mission has been in motion long before time began. As we have said already, there was a time when there was perfect harmony in not only the world but in the universe.

Self always wants to exalt itself above others, so Lucifer, the high ranking angel and the bringer of light, in the very presence of the most holy in the Ancient of Days, became full with self. No human language can describe this type of discontent. He referred to Lucifer as perfect, until evil was found in him, the mystery of it all. Come and behold the master plan in motion. The Eternal most merciful takes pleasure in the happiness of man. Selfishness and the ego only bring separation, and this lack in the nature of humanity will only produce greed, violence and unhappiness. The Eternal will stop at nothing to ransom humanity.

The rebellion against the Eternal most holy, His order and His divine law, started in heaven—the third heaven, the very dwelling place of the most high—and that rebellion, self-ego, came to the Earth later, as we will see as we travel in our discourse.

Lucifer, who was perfect and had no lack, became selfish. Our three dimensional brain or mind in our human state cannot explain who someone is in the very presence of the most gracious One. The Eternal permitted Lucifer this privilege to worship Him, but Lucifer, who made himself into the devil, Satan, became proud and selfish, and everything changed. We have said it before that once a person finds "a self," the possibility exists that the self will want to exalt itself above others.

Self or selfishness is our largest enemy, even in the third heaven. It was Lucifer who made himself into a devil's biggest problem, and on this planet, the ego is our largest problem. So in reality, the first rebellion as it remains stated, started in heaven. Rebellion always begat the rebelling Lucifer, who now is the devil Satan. This name change now denotes a different character, as there is a lot in a name. His name was changed to Satan, the deceiver, adversary and accuser of the people.

Evil has influenced one negatively, so the devil starts to influence other angelic hosts. Let's back up a little. The real target of this devil is the seat of power, the Eternal most gracious and the very throne of the universe itself; so the first tactic of the evil one is to create doubt in the angelic host. This is basically the same tactic that is used in today's cosmos or world to defame others for selfish gain. We can blame the devil for this one, but we have to stop blaming the devil for everything, and we have to take responsibility. So the real target of the evil one is the Eternal Most Holy himself. Please do not forget that we have said it before, that this is of utmost importance: that our biggest enemy is the self. This goes to the root cause of all our problems.

In the evil one's presence, he was perfect until evil was found in him—ego. We cannot overemphasize this point where there is self-ego, and all of us humans, to a greater or lesser degree, have ego and selfishness in our nature. Every divine order that the most merciful put in place is to help us to preserve self, because the Eternal knows that this selfishness will destroy us.

The Eternal most highest is not created. Lucifer, whom the good Lord created for His good pleasure, to delight in worshipping the most high, by this permission became disgruntled, and started to target the Creator, the most holy himself. I ask the question, what would you do in this situation? Do you think, in human concept, that the Eternal was challenged? Not at all; you just have to remember who the Eternal is—holy glory is His most gracious name. The Eternal always takes pleasure in forgiveness, and the Eternal's nature is love everlasting.

The first act of duality at play as we know it—the Creator, the most holy—is the creation of Lucifer, who made a devil out of himself, at war, spiritually speaking, with the all-powerful One, who is full of power, who will win love and will win justice. The Eternal, who is just and holy and full of power, could destroy the evil one in a moment, but He did not. He, the most holy, is full of wisdom, and all dictators can learn a lesson from this.

The Eternal, whose strength knows no bounds, and who is boundless and puts law and divine order in motion, does not violate His law himself, and He is justified in doing so instead. Praise and holy is He, the Eternal who appealed to Satan's mind to choose life instead of rebellion.

Inspiration tells us that the one who is perfect in knowledge, *glory to the highest*, appealed to Satan to change his rebellion and accept the tender caring mercies of the Eternal government, the other divine that always brings peace and happiness. It has been said that the evil one, Satan, after the loving appeal of the most merciful, almost came to repentance; but remember, almost saved, in reality, means forever lost. It is said that pride and selfishness stand in the way; that is how dangerous selfishness is. All of us humans need to apprehend this issue of the self, and rush for our own good sake.

To the Holy One, blessed be He to help us to surrender this self-ego by obeying divine order of authority, whatever they are. It is insane for us humans, after so many examples, to continue to rebel against the divine order that was designed for our good pleasure by our most merciful Creator.

The Eternal is so holy, He has to deal with this rebellion that the one who became Satan started. There are many people who blame the Eternal for creating sin and Satan's rebellion. Remember, all of the Eternal's creation includes the angels and man, and it was decreed before the foundation of the world that free choice would be the way the most gracious One would govern. We choose to obey or rebel, and that is our privilege; the Eternal, in His mercies, give us this right. He accepts worship only from free choice produced from love.

## The Origin of Rebellion

By all accounts, the beginning of rebellion did not start on planet Earth, but it started in the upper world, the third heaven, in the very presence of the most high. Remember when we started in Genesis, the beginning; I did remind us that there are several beginnings. We have the beginning of the beginning, and we have the beginning of the Creator in the case of the Eternal; there is no such thing as a beginning of time, space or matter. So it is clear that rebellion, which is sin, has its beginning in heaven, in a blissful atmosphere. This makes it more difficult to apprehend how or why this rebellion started in Lucifer's mind. It is called the mystery of sin.

We humans do not have to worry about why rebellion started in the first place. We should just pause at this moment and ask the most merciful for His good favour, to make the best choice to obey His divine order; and they are good for us: good health, peace and happiness. We cannot buy these favours with things, money or toys, as these blessings are gifts to us through and by the most holy favour.

So the rebellion started in the upper world, and then before we knew it, the rebellion started in another location—the new Earth. On this planet Earth, it originally began in the north, not the west. The Earth has four corners, like many things on the planet. So the rebellion got started in the north, which the holy book called Eden, which really means pleasure and paradise.

It must be made abundantly clear that the most loving Eternal did not cast out the devil on this planet Earth to torment us humans. There are some people who have this insane thought. We should know by now that we humans are not the only ones in our universe, as there are many other planets with inhabitants. Inspiration tells us that the evil one, the devil, was cast out of the presence of the most Holy One, who will not tolerate sin and rebellion forever. That is a warning for all the inhabitants of the Earth.

It has been said that the devil visited many other planets, but did not receive any response to his deception and rebellion, and he finally touched down on this planet Earth. I can hear all the skeptics, like the scientists, philosophers and anthropologists, laughing that this concept does not make any sense, but they are the first to laugh and will not be the last. It has been said that the simplest thing is the most profound ever in nature, and even the simple language is the most profound. Now we see how the rebellion (evil) started or had it's beginning on planet Earth. The pronouncement to the inhabitants of the Earth was because the evil one has gone down, and his time is short, and we will soon run out. Regardless of how the evil one, the devil, pretends to be powerful, he is not. He is a created being and is confined to time and space. On the other hand, or in contrast, the only true reality in the entire universe is the most holy, most true one of the divine order, which is that the Eternal alone is sovereign over all and in all, there in the upper world, heaven, and Earth, His footstool.

In the beginning, the Eternal, God, created the heavens and the Earth. Now we know that the war, rebellion and sin started in heaven, and now it begins on Earth, and we will see quickly that it is going to get vicious and violent.

## First Human Family in Eden

The rebellion began on Earth, and the holy book gives us an idea where on Earth it took place. That land still exists today; it is between some rivers. This is where the holy book gives this piece of real estate a name for the first time—it is called "Eden." Where two of the most important rivers are, the Tigris-Euphrates and the River Nile, is where Eden is located. Without water, we cannot live. These rivers donate the tender loving care of the Eternal most gracious.

On Earth, we see Eden, a land mass in North Africa. Look for the river Nile, and you cannot be mistaken where this place is. This land is still there today, but of course has different names in the different regions it flows through. Some call it the Middle East. What is very interesting is that this land Eden is where the Eternal most wise chose to start the human family tree, and this is now where some of the first wars have been being fought, by war perpetrators like Britain and America. This is also where the first rebellion started on this Earth, by the one who made a devil out of himself.

Eden means pleasure or paradise, in North Africa. The garden is not Eden; the garden was *in* Eden, a land mass with rivers and gardens. This might sound like heaven to you as a human, and this is the place everyone wants to be. Well, the Eternal, in His wisdom, started the human family right here in Eden, or Africa if you please, in the garden that was Eden, by the river Nile. The human family started with two dualities, a divine order of "opposite attracts," so the most all-knowing created the man and woman, male and female, principles. This is a very important divine order, and this is an unchangeable principle for the development of the family. Therefore, no human can or has the right to violate this divine order, male and female, as He created them. In this eternal context, same sex marriages have no moral or legal standing, regardless of what the courts or the people in the world wish. The male and female principles are in all facets of life and creation, and cannot be changed with time or place.

We are still discussing the rebellion that started in the upper world and how it is playing its ugly self on Earth, in partiality in the garden that is Eden (North Africa), where the Eternal most holy created the first family, the man and woman. Inspiration tells us that the Eternal instructed them, where making correct choices in life was concerned, against Lucifer who became Satan. This human couple had the freedom to choose and were forewarned to be careful to choose to obey the loving Lord with all their mind and strength, just like us humans today. We have the freedom to obey or disobey, but just like the law of nature, for every action, there is an equal reaction. As it has been said before, the cause is in the effect. So our earthly parents, in the Garden of Eden (North Africa), disobeyed the most Eternal loving One by listening to the evil one's deception.

The human family started dying ever since that moment. By disobeying, we disconnect ourselves from real life, spiritual, metaphysical principles, which means that in order to have real life, we have to be connected to the Eternal, spiritually speaking, by obeying all of His divine order.

Joshua 1 stated that without Him, we humans are nothing, and the first principle of biology is that life can only come from life. The only reality in the whole universe is the most gracious One, and we humans can only have real life if we are connected to Him. Temporal life is only fueled through carbon, oxygen and food, but that is not real life, and we can be transformed when we choose life, by connecting through or by choosing to obey the divine order of authority.

The greed, violence, unhappiness and stress we humans experience today is a direct or indirect result of the lack we have by rejecting the truth of sublime knowledge.

This lack is what we receive for wages; as the holy book stated, the wage for disobeying the divine orders is death.

## The Plan of Redemption

By disobeying, we separate ourselves from life itself. The absence of life is death, but the Eternal is the God of life, and he invites all of us to choose life. Furthermore, the Eternal most gracious initiated himself a masterpiece or "rescue plan" as it were. This is the most unbelievable and beautiful language that could fall on humans' ears: the "Redemptive Plan" to resave humanity.

Lucifer started his rebellion and, by now, you know that he is Satan, the deceiver. The war has shifted to our planet now and the human family, through our foreparents, who rejected the Eternal's will that would have given them life forever.

Come and behold what kind of love this is: Humanity rejected the most gracious mercies, and the Eternal himself is so moved, humanly speaking, that He, the Eternal, is about to give himself for ransom for these people. ***What love (amour) is this!!***

The Eternal, in His love, extends the same favours to Lucifer, who is now the devil, that now extends to our foreparents, to reject self-rebellion, greed and violence, and receive His mercies, favour and grace, which will produce life, real happiness, giving and sharing.

The principle of sharing is one of the divine orders that the Eternal gives us, to help starve selfishness and greed so that true transformation can begin. We receive for the purpose of sharing and, by giving, we start living. The only thing we keep is what we give away.

It is in this context that the holy book teaches that it is better to give than to receive, so the Eternal most giving lives this way of sharing.

It remains stated that the Eternal most holy was so full of love that He gave himself. And the Eternal Father is the Father and the Son; the Eternal Son Yeshua, the Christ, is beloved Father and Son. The spirit of the Eternal is both the Father and the Son.

The word "God" is not a singular word, but it is a family name. *Hear O Israel: your Lord, the Lord, is one.* Human concept of mathematics is different from the Eternal. The digit "1" can mean infinity in a certain grade of digit mathematically. Because we humans count in sequence (1, 2, 3), we generally think the number 1 is more important than the number 3.

In the beginning of our discussion, we make it very clear that no human language can express or describe the high and lofty One.

So when we use the expression or the word "God," we refer to a family name, and there are different personalities in the GodHead. "Eternal" is a human expression and is not final in the description of the most holy. The expression "God (or Eternal) gave His son" has to be apprehended in the correct context. In the book Psalms, it is expressed that there was an arrangement established with the Eternal, traced in the distant past, that the family of the Eternal One will redeem humanity most lovingly. *What love is this!!*

So when we read in the holy volume, "for God so loved the world," the expression really means "the Son so loved the world that He gave himself." God so loved the world that He gave himself, and remember that the Eternal most holy has no gender, so the expression or word "He" is a human expression.

In reality, the Eternal most merciful is self-existing and cannot be begotten or begat. To ransom humanity from rebellion, only the

Eternal, who has life inherently, can give. Life can only come from life, and cannot come from nonliving, so no angels, regardless of rank, could ransom humanity. It takes someone with real life in them to give life, so the Eternal gave life—the Eternal gave himself—and this type of love cannot be expressed or apprehended by mortals.

This is the reason the apostle John, in the holy book, just has to make a proclamation to all of creation in heaven and on Earth to "come and behold what love is this." To buy back man from destruction, the Eternal, the most noble, devised a master plan amongst the Eternal family as a team effort. Humanly speaking, each one will play a role in this rescue mission; this is a divine order and arrangement amongst the God or Eternal family.

To save humans, remember we are not angels as yet, as we were made a little lower than the angels, just for a while, as stated in the holy book. Just imagine for a moment that the Eternal most vast, in many actions, transcends space to save man from himself, and based on spiritual law has to become a human himself. We cannot apprehend this though, but it was His will.

We should know by now that human beginnings started in a lowly state, as just moist earth or clay, and that is a humble start if you ask me. In this moist clay, our awesome bodies were incubated, and the most gracious One created from earth, but not just to remain earthly, but with awesome ability. He, the Eternal, most sublime all-knowing, chose to invest himself in us humans. This is the sweetest, oldest story in the whole wide world—the wonderment of the ages that the Eternal of all ages became a human to purchase us himself, so that we can have eternal life, in exchange for selfishness, greed, pride and ultimate death. *This is supremely good news!!*

Life can only come from life, so it remains stated in the holy volume that the good Lord provides a human body for himself and becomes a man—by one man, all men die. The duality: By one man being alive, all men have received eternal life. The first man in Eden, Adam, brings death, while the second, Yeshua himself, brings life.

Let us now recap and share a thought for a moment. We recall a moment in time when there was total harmony: Everything pulsated in worship to the most Holy One, but suddenly there was a missed beat or disharmony. This was not a surprise to the Eternal, as He is all-knowing, the One who is described metaphorically with many eyes. The eternal being is the only sovereign One who cannot be surprised, but He permits certain things to happen for His plan, being all wise. We humans blame the Eternal for everything; we stated before that we cannot blame the Eternal when we choose the wrong path.

As discussed before, Lucifer, who became Satan, chose to rebel against the Eternal most loving, who appealed to his mind to give up his rebellion, but he refused. Being the most holy there in the upper world, heaven, Satan was removed. The Eternal is the only rightful ruler of the universe, but it is an insane idea that the good Lord threw Satan onto Earth to tempt us. The most holy cannot tempt us, and if you recall, the Lord's Prayer said, *"Lead us not into temptation,"* which is a misleading reading; the correct reading should be, *"We must ask the good Lord not to permit our trials to us."*

So the evil one arrived on Earth, and our human foreparents were told at creation about the devil, the evil one. The most holy Lord must have told them to be aware and to make proper distinction. We know the rest of the story; our human parents rejected the loving master, and the human family has been rebelling ever since. So the Eternal most graceful took on human form and became a human himself. This is the type of love that is called the mystery of goodness supreme. One should not miss the pattern that the Eternal was painting when He started the first family tree on this planet Earth. He, the Eternal, chose to put the first human in Eden, also in South Egypt; this was by design.

When He, the Eternal, chose a body to condescend in human form to pay the ransom for humanity, again, by the sovereign choice of the only wise Eternal, North Africa was the chosen racial type of the duality—both man and woman were African. Do you think the decision of our Creator most gracious is a mistake?

## *The First Family on Earth was Nubian/African*

The most holy blessed be He, who by the sovereign choice decided to make the first two humans Nubian or African. Yeshua the Christ, who became human to save humanity from rebellion, was also a Nubian or African. I know for sure that a lot of people, both black and those of other branches of humanity who classify themselves as white, are boiling with anger. Both classified groups will argue that colour does not matter, so you ask why all the icons or expressions have changed in the holy book, to be pale skin, if colour does not matter. The fact of the matter is that colour and money is what runs this corrupt world or cosmos. In other words, the world order now is the ascendancy of racial hegemony and economic exploitation. The rest is mechanism and ways and means.

The only time it does not matter what colour Yeshua (Jesus) is, is when people behave humanely and are honest with themselves, and accept the facts based on evidence. I am not trying to prove anything to anyone. Go to the holy book and to the library, and do your own research, but you have to keep an open mind.

So we see the Eternal take on human form, which is unbelievable. This act is the wonder of all ages. As we try to write this narrative, we are going back and forth; keep in mind that there are different timelines in these events, so we are sometimes speaking in the past, present and future tense. My discussion is very condensed and concise, dealing only with points. So the reader has to do their own research or study, and that is one of my opinions, so I will give no dates or verses to go to. I am just writing about sequences of events as I study and apprehend these themes, and share concepts and ideas so that we can have open and objective discussions on all the important subject matter that have to do with the future of humanity on the planet. All of us will be affected by what goes on here below, so we better get started and talk to each other respectfully. As they say, we are in it together, and we belong together. Each to all, all to one another, we belong to each other. This is also a divine order of authority.

## The Eternal's Use of Numbers

The Eternal most holy, most loving, most kind, emptied heaven of all its treasure to redeem the human race. Humanity at this moment in time is in rebellion against the most gracious. The rebellion was so intense after the 7th generation (remember the perfect number). What I meant by that is that the Eternal is the supreme mathematician and is ever pulsating, and our universe is calibrated mathematically. So the Eternal most wise makes use of certain numbers, and 7 is one of those numbers (7 days in a week; 7 plagues or place of the Earth), along with 3,12, 5 and many others. The true God or Eternal gave us our 5 senses, the 12 gates in the city and so on.

There was a new beginning again after 7 generations. The Eternal himself stated that the rebellion on the Earth was so intense that each, through the imagination of the people of that time, were only evil constantly. Again, the Eternal was not caught by surprise. Through cause and effect, again man was made perfect, but he had to choose to either follow the Eternal's divine order or rebel, and he chose the latter.

Rebellion only begets rebellion, then and now, and the most loving One always entreats and encourages humanity to change for the better. The Eternal has to, humanly speaking, respect the choice of rebellion that the people make out of His love, but He has to put an end to evil because He is so holy, and it is for the good of those who rebelled. You see, if rebellion, selfishness, greed and violence are left by themselves, negative energy and self-destruction will result. So even if the good Lord left humanity by themselves to rebel, they would ultimately destroy themselves and would cause more suffering. The Eternal, even at this moment in time, is saving us from ourselves. We have, on Earth at this moment, enough nuclear bombs to destroy all of us together.

The Eternal most merciful is saving us from ourselves at this moment. That is the reason we state at the beginning of our little discussion that self-greed is the most dangerous, and the Eternal has to deal with this human nature of selfishness. The lack in the self is the root cause of rebellion and greed.

After pleading with man for 7 generations—this is from the beginning, when the first pair of humans was created in Eden, North Africa, so it is true that both good and bad started with the Nubian—the Eternal has to deal with evil in the same way that He has to deal with the rebellion in heaven, with the one who made a devil out of himself, Lucifer. It has been said that one of the strangest acts of the most gracious One is that He has to destroy evil for the good of humanity. We have two actions: one of the divine order, and the order of duality; one below, one above, and the heavens above open up, and it starts raining. The holy book calls it the deluge or the flood.

The Eternal, most full of power, or powerful, makes all things new and beautiful, and the first human family tree started with two duality, male and female principles. Please take note, these two humans of African origin, Adam and Eve (or Evette), people, this Earth or the planet, until the 7th generation and then after the deluge (flood), the Eternal most merciful started another beginning, to populate the Earth with eight humans, Noah's family.

An encouraging thought is that all through human history, there were always a few people or a nation that chose to follow the Eternal path always. Remember, duality is a part of the divine order. There are two ways, and one path is straight, which means that it is difficult and narrow. The self-ego, the self, is always rebelling. It will take our whole lifetime to tame or discipline the self. The broad path is easy to navigate or walk and is natural to the self. You have to make a choice to reverence your maker, the Most High; it is for our good reason.

The very same way Eternal makes use of certain numbers in His providence, like the number 7 (7 days in a week, 7 heavens, 7 plagues of the Earth), is why I personally believe 2007 was a very interesting time on the Eternal's mathematical clock. Time begins with humans; a thousand years is like a day to the most gracious. He has no concept of time like humans do. The only time we really have as humans is only a heartbeat away, and we take in oxygen a breath at a time. We humans are very arrogant; we behave as if we have all the time in the world. As I think about our behaviour, and how we think independently of the Eternal, puffed up, I conclude that we are really insane for sure.

## Law and Mathematics (the Purpose of Law)

We have spoken on this subject matter before, but because it is so important and profoundly essential, we have to speak to the subject again. The Eternal governs His vast multi-universe through His law, and the purpose of law is to promote order, harmony and balance. No one would disagree that we need the stop signs on the road, as you know already that there would be a lot of accidents without them. What about the law of gravity; do we need that law? You know that without the law of gravity on Earth, all of us would be floating in mid-air. So where this madness of the idea comes from, that we do not need the law anymore, is a mystery.

Some religious people even go as far as saying that the law was nailed to the cross. What law is nailed to the cross? The ceremonial law of sacrificing lambs for the remission of sins was nailed to the cross, not the moral laws of the Ten Commandments. My observation is that most of the "hocus pocus" nonsense comes from the religious world. The secular society seems to be more current on the purpose of the law, and they seem to apprehend that there are different types of laws.

People with a conscience, professional people, know that there are different types of laws that govern this multi-universe, and that our Creator made laws for the benefit of mankind. It is the people who crucified Yeshua (Jesus) as Christian religious who chose not to uphold the different types of laws, and remain not in the dark but allegiance.

Remember, darkness is a supreme state that the eternal God divided before He created light.

The law of health, traffic laws, the law of gravity, the law of darkness and light—our body is governed by many laws: the law of the mind. The sovereign Eternal, who has no counsel, uses all His laws to govern, supervise and rule this universe, and for frail, weak human beings to want to instruct the sovereign One, is the height of madness. This is what we as humans are trying to tell the Lord to do. We must stop this insanity.

What we must do today, as human beings, is to ask the most merciful, full of mercy, to forgive us, and He will if we humble ourselves and pray. The eternal takes pleasure in forgiving His people, His creation—unlike us humans who like to hold grudges.

Indeed, the ceremonial law of killing doves and lambs by our ancestors is no longer applied. Why? Because Yeshua (Jesus) came and purchased us with His royal pure blood. The author is overjoyed that Yeshua died for him, and with the wonder of it all. Do not ask me to explain this type of marvel and wonderment. This book is about divine order. Remember, order means law. Rebellion against our Creator is why this planet is reeling out of order. Now, the apex, the moral of the story and what we have been talking about, is this: The law of gravity applies today, and the law of health applies today—and please remember that these laws are living; they are not static. If we break them, they will break us, and if the truth be told, we would admit to ourselves that the law we want to get rid of is the moral law of the Ten Commandments.

Remember the pyramid text that our ancestors wrote on the wall of that great sarcophagi. It remains written that we must be true to ourselves. The pyramid text goes like this: "This mankind knows themselves and to thyself be true." Again, if truth be told, a lot of people, even church people who should know better, out of their concern and selfishness, even the rebellious, want to get rid of the law of the Ten Commandments, and in particular the fourth commandment. The commandment about the Sabbath is the only one that commands all of us on the planet Earth, to remember to keep the Sabbath holy.

Please remember that the moral law of the Ten Commandments cannot be changed, as they were given to humanity for our good. Like the laws of health and gravity, they are designed by the Creator for our good and protection. They cannot be changed, and the law of the Ten Commandments is immutable, as we have stated before. The Eternal governs His vast multi-universe through His laws, the law of nature, whereas the moral Ten Commandments have to do with our spiritual life and morality, and building character not just for this life but for eternity. We need to sit back up and pay attention as individuals and as a nation, because when it comes to your and my character, thoughts and emotions, only the moral law can deal with the intent and intentions. All through this book, we will continue to emphasize the absolute importance of the moral law that will be there, and which stitches this book together.

The Creator uses law and mathematics, as a part of His divine order to govern His vast multi-universe, for balance. We as humans will not be able to qualify many things mathematically because of the boundary of our minds (and our minds do have a boundary), designed by our Creator not to keep any good thing away from us but for our protection. On the other hand, the Most High and Lofty makes use of the law of mathematics and, every day, everything in His universe, where He rules as the sovereign on high, glory to El Shaddai, and is the only one who can justify everything mathematically.

All-knowing, all-wise and invisible—that is whom we as humans have to deal with, and have to give account and be accountable.

I trust we are all paying attention lest we forget. Nothing escapes the Eternal, and He pays attention to details. The all-knowing One doesn't use mathematics to inform himself as humans do. The sovereign One keeps record, as we have said before, and we are saying it again; the Eternal and all-knowing keeps record mathematically because He cannot lie, and He is not a man. He keeps the record because He knows that He cannot lie, not to prove anything to anyone. He can only prove to himself, as no one is greater than He, so the Eternal keeps the record mathematically for us, the untold universe, to wonder at for all eternity, and for anyone who dares to accuse the Holy One of Israel, here on this planet Earth or anywhere else in the vast universe. We know that there is always someone somewhere trying to take advantage of someone, to accuse, but not this time. The righteous Holy One is so original, so precise and so particular that no one can bear false witness against the Holy One. So our dear Lord and Saviour mathematically qualified in His record, in His book of remembrance, each and every one of us.

He (God) knows how many breaths we take during our lifespan on this Earth.

The Eternal once asked one of our ancestors a few questions. His name was Job, a very noble man, and his story remains written in the Book of Job. This Book of Job is one of the oldest books in the Bible. One of the questions the Lord most gracious asked Job was if he knew where the storeroom of the soul is. All the muscles in Job's body rearranged themselves, and he was astonished and put his finger over his mouth in silence. We all must learn from Job's attitude and stop trying to teach the all-wise One and be silent before Him. Even the hair on our head is numbered mathematically. The Eternal so loves us, with an everlasting love, and that is why He is so particular with so much detail. We are His royal priesthood. He has invested His very life in us, with priceless, boundless and unbounded love, love that will not let me go. Mercy said no! I trust that humanity will heed the call. This is the utmost purpose of this book.

## Mind over Matter (the Wonderment of the Brain)

One of the marvels of creation is the brain, the seat of the centre of the body and mind. Even if we discuss this subject matter a thousand million times, we still know almost nothing about the brain and the mind. Even the most fertile neuroscientists, cosmologists and spiritualists still only know very little about how the brain works. These neuro-specialists tell us that we only use a small fraction of our brain power. I am speaking to any authority on the subject of the brain/mind. We know our brain is in the little cap of our head at the frontal lobe, with some soft tissues of billions of neurons connected wirelessly at a high speed of energy. Remember, we are not talking about our "5G" internet. We are actually talking about our brain/mind, the most powerful thing ever created by our Creator the eternal God.

If you notice, I use the word brain/mind interchangeably because the mind is beyond words, and because the mind emanates from the brain. We can agree on this one truth, not the fact that this cosmic world or Earth system of things is in us. Crime and violence is everywhere, families are breaking up and many preteens and young adults are in confusion. There is lack of trust of citizens in the government, violence is rampant in school, and seniors and teachers are not respected. This is a signal of the home, in kids; all of the above problems we are discussing start in the brain/mind. Remember, the seat of control of everything starts in the mind.

If the mind/brain is what controls our whole body and our behaviour, this chain of thought is of utmost importance. If we have to change our minds first through the brain, this is where the real work challenge begins; the battle is for our minds. Who and what controls our minds, controls us. I do not have to tell you that it is not a simple or easy thing to control our minds. This subject matter is not even understood; whenever we start to discuss things of the mind, we have already shifted into another dimension, spiritually speaking.

We are living in an age of mental diseases. All of us humans are touched by some kind of mental disorder, some more than others. Some people may think and say, "How dare you say that all of us have some kind of mental health issue." Let us just talk about it together. If truth be told, most of us, if not all of us, do not like to talk about mental health. It is just reasonable that anything to do with the brain/mind is very complex. You, the reader, know that much. The writer or author is under no illusion about the subject matter, but we have to talk about the subject of the mind. You do not have to be a rocket scientist.

I will be the first to tell you that I, the author/writer, have no special training of the mind. I see myself as an observer bearing witness to this phenomenon called the mind, and I am sharing the concept about this great wonder, the masterpiece of all of the Creator's creation, and even as I pen these words, I am still in a state of wonder at the wonder of the mind.

## Where Does the Mind Dwell?

Like everything the eternal God created, there is a line of divine order to follow as His creation; to get the correct results, there are always set procedures and precautions to follow. Almost everyone drives nowadays; whether it is a good thing or a bad thing, the environmental scientist is still looking into this. It will still be better for us to talk some more; it is good for us, but the point I am trying to make about the vehicle is that the maker of that SUV gives you a manual with the vehicle, to follow. You know what will happen if you do not follow that manual; you will have to spend a lot of money. So the mastermind of the multi-universe, our kind loving Creator who created our brain/mind, gives us some procedure protocol or drive order to protect our minds and keep them in good mental health. In the holy volume, it remains written, and the instruction is that we must guard our minds with diligence; in front of it, our minds come to the issue of life.

One of the reasons we have so many mental health issues in our world today is that we do not guard our minds about what we think and look at. So the big question is, what is the main cause of most mental illnesses? Such a complex issue has many reasons, but based on my observations, there are two main reasons why there are so many mental issues. Always remember, this is not a simple, aimless question; therefore, if a human being does not have a purpose in life, why were they born?

Where are things going in life? Why was the universe created, and why do bad things happen to good people? These are good fundamental questions that need answers, if a person does not have a correct balanced answer to these questions. I always try to share in my conversations that if a person does not have to cast opposition about a subject matter, such a person is in confusion or dwells in superstition. If one dwells in that zone too long, then confusion will take over the mind, and that can lead to a nervous breakdown. Then mental illness starts to set in, and some people can get treatment and become whole again or well. Some may have a more difficult time healing. Your best asset and investment is to maintain a healthy mental state. As you read through this book, you will notice that I repeat for emphasis issues through concepts, so that our long-term memory can intercept the idea. We are trying to share, as our dear Saviour and Lord stated, that He remembers that our memory is short, so mercy is extended. So let us remind ourselves of the title of this book: *Divine Order of Authority.*

That title means something if you observe carefully. We stated at the beginning of this book that the Eternal governs His vast universe through laws that He put in motion even before He created this round green Earth. So another word of law is order. Political procedures help to operate in law and order so it is very important that we as humans observe the eternal God protocol and procedure. I visited the court a lot of times, and I observed that if you do not file your documents properly following the rule of procedure, even if you are in the right, the judge can throw out your case if you did not file your case and follow the right procedure. If a sinful judge can throw out our case if we did not follow the law of procedure, what about the Holy One of Israel and glory?

It remains written in the holy volume that it is a terrible thing for any man, or woman for that matter, to fall in the hands of the Lord. It has been said in another place in the book that the spirit of the Eternal will not always strive with man or mankind. Even in another place, the

Holy One of Israel stated that anyone that takes His name in vain will not be held guiltless. This is the most merciful speech here. So as children of Adam and all of humanity, let us take the Lord seriously and at His Word. He, the Lord most gracious, gives us in His Word, His law, protocols and procedures to follow for our good. Whatever the Eternal asks us to do is for our good, not for Him the Eternal, as we stated before and are saying again. The Lord most gracious has no need whatsoever, no lack; even if the Lord asks us to do something and, in our human eyes, it does no good for us, it is good for us. The Lord wishes above all things that you all will prosper and be in good health even as you prosper spiritually.

One of the divine orders, laws and protocol procedures is the family, which was created from the beginning—a man and woman for company and complement. If someone—an individual, a group or a nation—does not agree with that principle, they need to talk to the Creator on this matter, who made it so for balance and our good and a purpose. So don't gossip with me on this subject matter, as this is a divine arrangement.

Another divine order is that a day consists of darkness and light. Darkness was created before light. The most Holy One stated that He the Eternal cover himself with shame, darkness. Nothing is said negatively about darkness here; this negative concept comes from and was created by evil-minded people. This evil started in different places in the world but was perpetrated by the British. As COVID-19 is international, so is systemic racism. Racism was constructed, so it can be deconstructed. It was designed by some to make profit from the suffering of others, and that is criminal.

So what is blackness? Blackness is a supreme state in which the Eternal (God) dwelled in before He created light. All colours melt into blackness; therefore, all colours come from blackness. Blackness is not a colour, and neither is whiteness. Whiteness means blank or void of colour. That is a divine order. Another divine order, protocol or procedure is how to pray, and if we have never prayed before, now is the time for real prayer. As the old Negro spiritual song says, "It's me, it's me, oh Lord, standing in the need of prayer. It's not my mother or father, but it's me, oh Lord, standing in need of prayer." The model, our master teacher Yahweh, taught us to pray. We call it the Lord's Prayer, but it is actually the disciple's prayer.

"Our father, who art in heaven, praise worthy is your name"—you notice that our master teacher is invoking the oneness of each other. He did not say "my Father" but "our Father." With this principle, if we are not careful, we might gloss over what the master teacher is trying to teach us. The oneness is emphasized by our master teacher, Yeshua Hamashiach (some call Him Jesus and that is also fine), who is our shalom. In this one sentence, Yeshua negates the idea that your God is better than your neighbour's God. This may sound like a simple matter, but this concept is what is creating all the violence and war on this planet. If we see ourselves in each other, that one concept can stop a lot of the violence, whether religious, racism or other types of bigotry, because these wars and violence are predicates of the idea that my God is better than yours. "Hallowed be thy name, praiseworthy is thy name." The name of the Lord must be held in utmost reverence, and no man or woman should be called reverend. The Lord said of himself, "Reverence and holy is my name, and I share my glory with none." I have heard a lot of prayers that I would describe as taking the Lord's name in vain. We should stop repeating the Lord's name over and over in our prayers. We must ask the Lord prayerfully to teach us to pray all over again, and listen. The author is speaking to himself also. Let us start to see with our eyes and hear with our ears the Word; in His wisdom, He gave us two ears, two eyes and one mouth. Let's talk less and do more; be still and know.

I must speak a little on this all-important divine order, the Sabbath. The Lord himself set this example for us humans, all humanity, not the jewel or SDA. This sacred day for mankind is to benefit us for our good, not the Lord's; He is Lord, sovereign of the Sabbath. He created us and knows our short memory, so He, the sovereign One, reminds us to remember the Sabbath day and to keep it holy, meaning we must remember to hallow those hours as sacred; both in the Old Covenant and the New Covenant, the Lord most gracious asks us to keep His Sabbath day holy. From one Sabbath to another, shall all human families come to Mount Zion to worship their Creator.

## Law of Mathematics

We have been trying to share with you, the reader, that the creator, the Eternal, governs and rules His vast multi-universe, including planet Earth, through His prime principles of law and mathematics. We are not discussing the law of mathematics itself, or the properties or fundamentals of what actually constitutes mathematics itself. That is a principle that would take up the whole book. What we are doing together is apprehending (understanding) the real purpose of the law of mathematics and how the Eternal (God), our Creator, uses the law of mathematics to govern His creation. Just like light, mathematics is not easy to define. Just think for a moment. Can you, the reader, define time as a science? Time is difficult to define, if it can be defined.

As human beings on this planet, my observation is that we do nothing about these things very much. We are working and trying to understand our iPhones. You know that I am not implying that work is not important. What I am actually saying is that we spend our lifetime on these things and neglect to observe God's creation and the laws that govern it. Do you know that this green Earth that you are standing on at this moment is rotating or spinning around the sun at an unrecognized speed, which our consciousness cannot recognize? Just because our conscious mind cannot see it happening, it does not mean we should think that the Earth is standing still. Seeing is not believing; knowing is what is of the utmost importance.

Nothing is standing still; everything in the universe vibrates. That is a divine order, and just because you are not seeing or bearing witness, it doesn't mean it is not happening. Certain things in creation are too important to see. Most of the things we see are not as they actually are. Remember the optical illusion. You have two types of illusions, one of which are positive illusions, like the light that reflects from the sun to the moon. That light, as cool as it is, affects the waves on that massive body of water called the sea. The negative illusions can get all of us sick, even some with mental problems. The causation of these illnesses can be traced back to the negative illumination that our monkey-minded minds keep telling us horror stories in our thoughts, which do not exist. But we still frustrate ourselves over these negative things that cause us a lot of stress and fear. That is why our loving and most merciful, full of mercy, calls us to be still and to know—not believe but to know—that He is the "Isness." So, we will be going back and forth in our little dialogue. That is how the forces of life actually work. Back and forth, in and out, we went all through the narration, just for us to have a better appreciation (understanding).

By observing the great works of our Creator, and applying the law of mathematics, all of us, as humans, will grow to appreciate, worship, honour, respect, adore and extol our dear Saviour and Lord, forever and ever and ever. Amen.

We come to realize that everything in the universe vibrates or spins at different frequencies and speeds. Have you ever wondered why it is important to know that your Creator, and mine, created all the things we see and all the massive invisible universe? It is equally important for us also to try to make the effort to apprehend (understand) why the Lord created the things He did. Why two eyes and one mouth? Why did He create darkness or blackness? Why cold and hot? Why woman and man? All of creation is part of the divine order. Why do you think so? Do not answer; just be still, and think how the Lord most merciful stated in the holy book that He knows mathematically how many hairs you and I have on our head, and think about why the sovereign one goes out of His way to mention that He is qualified mathematically. How many stars are in the heavens? What about the heartbeats of your whole life? The Lord has already counted and knows how many heartbeats and breaths we take, and it is written, not because the all-wise creator can forget but because He can never forget, and it shows us humans how meticulous and organized our great Creator is. He has no lack of memory like us humans, and we humans do not even wait to write them down; we are really lazy. Everything the Lord does, He wants to make it a teachable moment for our good. I trust we have started seeing how important the law of mathematics is, and how the eternal God uses mathematics and all His other laws to govern or rule His creation for order and harmony.

When you stand on this Earth, it looks flat—remember that we stated earlier that nothing looks the way it appears. So although it looks flat when you are standing on it, once you get into a spacecraft or are airborne, and you reach the top of this Earth's hemisphere and look down on the Earth, you will see a phenomenon. Even the people who orbit in space and look at the planet Earth, will tell you that seeing the Earth from that vantage point is one of the greatest experiences and one of the greatest wonders to them, to see that the Earth that they live on is in orbit and spinning.

While these astronauts were exploring, one exclaimed out loud—I think it was Neil Armstrong—with such a wonderment at seeing this green looking ball in orbit; it was something to behold. We, as laymen (people), are not astronauts, and we do not have thousands and thousands of US dollars to take a space trip—like Elon Musk, who was thinking about building a spaceship to take tourists into space. Most of us have to wait until the great "getting up morning." Glory!! So these astronauts look down from space and see a wonder: the round, green Earth spinning in orbit. "In orbit" really means hanging in space. They look down and remember that a few weeks ago, they were standing on Earth; now they are looking down at Earth. Do you apprehend the mystery of how your heavenly Father is wondrous in His creation (glory)? No wonder Neil Armstrong had to exclaim and say of the creator of the multi-universe, "Man, what a God."

So, the astronauts looked down to see the green Earth orbiting in space and were amazed at the wonder of their home planet Earth. I know that seeing what they saw, altered their lives forever. What I am trying to do is to thrust our brain-mind through its natural path so that we manage to see ourselves thinking outside the box, so to speak. When an engineer makes a bridge, mathematically, he has to calculate the weight distribution for the bridge he is building. The master engineer, the master mathematician, the master of all—don't you think that when He created this brand new Earth, at creation, He knew mathematically the weight of this Earth? As the Creator, the all-wise immortal invisible One, don't you think our Creator knew the weight of the Earth, and not only the weight but the possible weight that the Earth could hold until He returns to claim it and its inhabitants? It is in this context I am sharing the law of mathematics the Creator makes use of to rule and govern His last creation. The trees you see outside have the right amount of leaves according to that tree.

We do not give trees the right amount of respect, other than when we use them to build homes, and for cooking our food or for heat; we think little about these trees. In truth, we humans cannot live without trees. Trees help to keep us alive by giving us fresh oxygen, and in the next breath, through photosynthesis, exchanges the carbon dioxide into oxygen, and the cycle continues. They also protect the environment so that we don't have land erosion. Again, the most gracious, in His wisdom, put enough leaves on each tree. The law of mathematics applies here again: each tree, based on its type, has the right amount of leaves, mathematically speaking.

## Law and Mathematics

We have been having a dialogue on the subject of law, and on the law of mathematics. We have come to realize that in our communication, we observe and bear witness that our Creator made the law, and the law of mathematics, as part of His foundational principle. What is so surprising and a mystery is that our merciful, compassionate Eternal (God) observes and obeys His own laws, although He, the Elohim, has no lack or need whatsoever obey his own law. The most astonishing thing here is that we, as humans, who live by oxygen, by breathing one moment at a time, and who are weak in memory, chose not to obey the Lord's will, His law.

The holy law that our loving Creator created is for the good of every one of us and everything that breathes. With the correct knowledge and apprehension (understanding) of the true purpose of laws, we will realize that they are immutable for all time and beyond time. When we begin to look at law in the proper context, we will quickly realize that the moral law of life and many other laws will also apply in other universes, not only planet Earth.

Remember, in the title of the book, *Divine Order* (another word for law is order) is designed to keep the peace or order for that matter. In another place in the holy volume, it remains written that the eternal God is a God of order, not lawlessness; hence, we get that title "law and order." If mankind were following the law of our Creator, there would be peace in the land. Remember, man cannot make law. The Creator makes law and nature; God can make law. Man can make rules and regulations, not law. Even some of those rules and regulations that a city hall creates are good for us humans, like protecting the wetlands or picking up garbage (do not litter). How important are these regulations? Imagine the amount of chaos if the city didn't pick up our garbage. Let us suppose the city permitted littering, or cutting down any tree they wanted to cut down. All of a sudden, the weather pattern would have changed, the environment would be affected and there would be chaos with the unpredictable weather.

I am going out of my way to say how important the law of our Creator is, and the law of nature, to our existence. Now, after having this dialogue together, by now we must have a better appreciation for the principal purpose of law and mathematics, which is to create harmony and balance that regulates chaos. That is good for every one of us. Now we must observe if the law and the law of mathematics applies only to our planet, our solar system, or if the law of mathematics applies to many multi-universes beyond, and even to the very throne room of the incomparable, the unknowable, the sublime most righteous, the most holy. Glory!

Come and behold! The question is, does the law of the sovereign apply in the room of the utmost holiness in the stricter righteousness? Balancing agreeableness and total order, do laws apply in the ceremonies we say? Yes, the law still applies. We are seeing that the conflict of all the ages and the battle of the mind is about the law—the moral law of the Ten Commandments. Even in the holy of holiest, the law is needed, because the law always extends even before the fall of man. Another way to say it is when man sins or rebels against the law. The law is there for our protection. Just like the traffic rules, it is there to protect us from accidents, as are the moral laws and all the other laws in nature. They are there for our protection.

So, in the holy of holiest, where the eternal dwells, the holy law is there, and that is why we can say, because the law is a transcript of the Lord's character, the eternal God does not break His own law. He lives by His own law in His way of life and way of sharing, giving balance to the way of order, not disorder. The Lord most gracious wants us humans to live like Him, having no greed and not thinking only about ourselves but about others; that is how the Lord lives, thinking about others, His creation. In another place, it is written in His holy words that the Lord most gracious, stating about the people, only thinks of us just to do for us and to us. All things come of thee O Lord, and of thy own have we given thee. Amen. Glory.

## Humans Are Mysterious

The rebellion continued with all the entreatment from the most merciful Eternal, telling humanity to accept life, joy and peace, but men still continued to rebel. There's something of a mystery about us humans and our predisposition and disposition to reject life and happiness. This is not understood, and that is why I had to refer to such an attitude as insanity. The self-ego is an integral part of their rebellion, and self is our biggest enemy, and that is why the great call is to deny self and accept Yeshua's selfless life. Then and only then can we experience a real abundant life for the first time.

The desire to rescue must be for the purpose of sharing. By sharing, we starve ourselves, like when you have an apple to share with your friend. You cut the apple with one side bigger than the other. The natural thing is to take the bigger piece, as that is what the self wants. However, to love others like yourself is to give the bigger piece of the apple to your friend. By practicing this attitude, sharing becomes natural over time, and true happiness and transformation will start to take place. Then we will start to appreciate the principles that our good Lord teaches us. It is better to give than to receive.

*Come and behold this new thing.* The Eternal most merciful is about to do something new in the sense of dimensions. One of the divine orders of the Eternal's creation, including man, is to bring pleasure and beauty to himself, fully deserved as was stated before. He is the Holy One, and He gives us permission to worship Him out of His greatest love for our good pleasure, peace and happiness.

Remember, by good giving, we will receive; it is automatic.

The rebellion started in the upper world, heaven, and now it is raging on Earth. The first humans, from North Africa, in Eden, were also deceived by the evil one. They rejected God Eternal, and it does not matter who was deceived first, the man or the woman, as they both rejected the Eternal. It is important to note that one of the divine orders is that the man and the woman have different roles in the family; this is designed to create harmony. The difference here is for our benefit, but in the final analysis, the main responsibility is to protect the family for the good of all.

Rejection of the divine order, His laws, always creates chaos and ultimate death, so our first two human parents populated the Earth for up to seven generations, but in rebellion against the good Lord, 7 generations is a lot of time passed.

Remember the rescue mission we talked about before, in the supreme conference in heaven, in time infinity, between the most gracious Father Eternal and the most gracious Son, the most gracious spirit of the living that ever lived. The arrangement was made by the One who assumed the role of the Son, and the pay that will be received for sin and rebellion is death eternally. To reverse that law of divine order, the Eternal most merciful has to step in himself to rescue man from death eternally.

Governments of the world, arrogant people and ordinary people should pause and think, and if they really think about this thoroughly—the importance of the divine order of authority and how the Eternal views His law and divine order—then our human compassion will be changed.

The Eternal did not change His divine order; instead, when we were violated by human rebellion, the Eternal most gracious stepped in and gave himself to preserve the trust of the universe to maintain harmony and oneness. Once the division was made to pay the penalty of rebellion by the most holy triune God, a human body in time or in the future will be taken by the most Holy One. *Praise be He and exalted be His fame forever.* God cannot die, so He has to take a human body; the ransomed payment for sin and rebellion has to be said as the mystery of godliness. Do not ever think that your human language can decipher this greatness.

Again, that body was taken when the fullness of time came, by the Eternal sovereign choice in North Africa. Do not think for a moment it was by accident. This truth about the role of the Nubian father in all of history has to be told. Western Christianity has to back up and start to tell the truth about the role of the first human on the planet. The Son of God Eternal most Holy was slain in principle before the foundation of the world, to pay the ransom for the whole human race, starting from the Adamic, or first man, to the last man to be born in this age or present time. Yeshua the Christ, the God man, the divine order of duality—again now, we are in the world of contrast.

# You Are Sovereign. Think for Yourself. Let No One Think for You

The point to remember is that explaining something and defining it is totally different. To define anything, you first have to know its order and nature. For a long time, the matter of importance, such as who we are as human beings, was never defined to the people, yet it was explained away. As a result, the mass of the people remain in ignorance. The highest form of knowledge is self-knowledge; that is knowing who you are as a human being by nature. Go and visit the permitted text and read it again; man here is generic mankind. It remains written in the permitted text, "Man, know thyself, and to thyself be true." The time has long passed when we should depend on others to educate us, and it does not matter if it is your teacher at school, your pastor at church, your doctor or any other so-called expert.

I know that you, the readers, are intelligent enough to know that I am not implying that you should not listen to other people's points of view, including your teacher or pastor or a wise person. In fact, you should listen to everyone, but always use your own mind, logic, realization and apprehension; that is to say, you listen to each person with an open mind. It is critical here that you always reserve the right to think for yourself, and you must be free to think, and free to sense anyone, and I mean anyone, who does not give you the space to be free and does not have your interest at heart. By thinking for oneself, one can be fortified in that subject matter.

There are many professionals and so-called professionals who always think they should not be critiqued objectively, whether in politics, science, academia, religion or spirituality. A leader who wants informed people, needs to encourage them to question more.

Let's think for a moment that our Creator, who is all wise, all knowing, invites us to come and reason together. Can you believe that? The Creator is asking His people to come and reason together; in this case, in a dialogue. I think leaders today can learn from the example. Having a correct knowledge of self and self-discovery is one of the greatest needs of each person at this moment. This fact cannot be over emphasized if you have a real knowledge of self, knowing why you and I were created in the first instance by none other than the Eternal himself, and put on this planet for a mind expanding purpose. Once you have a correct knowledge of this master plan for your life, you will not want to commit suicide or even be confused anymore about your future and about why you were born. Instead, you will wake up every morning in love, giving gratitude for each moment of living.

We must always remember that the only time we all have is the moment of each breath we take, when we live in the past, the present and the future. It is no easy task, and this is our task to live in the moment. At school, when we were younger, if you recall, when the teacher called our name, we responded, "Present." Your response, when you say present, not only means that you are in attendance in person; it really means that you are paying attention, and that is to say that you are living in the moment. As I have said before, this is easier said than done. There are people who can live their whole lives and never be at home, which is to say that they never live in the moment with themselves. People are always immersed in compulsive thinking and mind chatting, which they call thought, but I call it "momentary" as most people never still their mind long enough to listen to their breathing. By not listening to the intelligence of our bodies, we destroy this marvelous body of ours; as truly, all human beings are walking marvels. We were created with awesome potential beyond our brain's boundary and ability to apprehend at this moment.

"Be still and know that I am."

## What Is Our Purpose?

Ultimately, our true potential and purpose is to develop into a true human being. A real human being is a person with intelligence and comprehension, and we are not human until we possess these qualities. *It is written and remains written that eyes have not seen, nor ears heard, nor does it enter into our minds what the good Lord has in store for us as human beings.* We essentially are the crowning act of His creation; His divine master plan is a sum. It will blow your mind, literally; that is to say, expand your brain cells as you think about your true purpose on this planet.

We ponder such things as why we were born, what God expects of us and where this world is heading. These are important questions, which are spiritual in nature, so you cannot go to your lab and do some experiments and get the answer to all these important matters. Self-discovery is the first requisite to success, be it physical or spiritual. When one has a true knowledge of oneself, simultaneously, you will know God, who will instruct you in the true path to which you must go, and then you will have no problem understanding your true purpose in life. One of the downfalls we have as human beings is that we allow other people to think for us.

Can you imagine that you are your own universe? Each one of us as human beings have billions of brain cells. As a universe with this same potential, how on God's Earth can you allow the greatest piece of invention on this planet—your brain, your mind—to be left to others to develop? You are the only one to be left with that responsibility. Always remember this expression: Use it or you will lose it.

There is some truth to that saying. Our brain is something like plastic. The expression, "blows your mind" or "expands your mind," is derived from this concept that the brain cells are elastic. By using your brain cells, they will expand, while on the other hand, if you leave them idle, they will go to waste. If you are into music and remember Lou Rawls, he is the artist who said that *"the mind is a terrible thing to be wasted."* We are our minds, and that is what each one is—the "Isness," the "Isness" of things—and your mind controls your body, so you are your brain. It is written and remains written in the holy volume, that is to say, holy fire or light in written word, that whatsoever a person thinks in his or her heart, so is he. The expression "... heart or mind, your whole life depends on it," is interchangeable.

Are you now getting why it is all important to apprehend how your brain works, and that your whole life depends on it? People say you are what you eat. I think there is some truth to that also, because if you do not eat proper foods such as lots of fruits, nuts and vegetables, and of course lots of quality water, your body cannot function, especially without water. Truth be told, your body is always after the water, so when you eat lots of fruits and vegetables, the body is not only after the nutrients but is after the water that naturally comes with food.

We are still on the subject matter of the brain, and this issue is so important that it could take up the whole book. Once you understand how the brain works, you have won a great part of the battle, and you will not be tricked by those horror stories and the confusion that your uncontrolled, compulsive brain will hurl at you. What is imperative for all of humanity at this moment in time, is to be still and start to observe your own thoughts and mind, and by doing so, you can disable or neutralize your negative thoughts.

Again, it remains written, the eternal speaking in the holy book, to be still and to know, be still in the mind and have stillness. If you notice, the Eternal did not say to be still and believe, but to be still and know that I am. Belief on its own cannot get you to this dimension; you have to know the nature of something and the order of things to say you know that thing. The wisest man that ever lived on this planet, the Nubian Moorish King Solomon the First, admonished us in Proverbs that we must guard our minds, our brains and our thoughts with much diligence because your very life depends on how you observe your own thoughts and guard your mind. As I said before, and I would like to emphasize it again, some people can live their entire lives and never be at home; that is to say that they never spend any time with themselves to even listen to their own heartbeat, and are unable to observe their inner thoughts. To go home and live at home is the ability to live with your natural self with total bliss.

The singer/songwriter, Bob Marley, wrote in one of his songs that we keep running away from ourselves, but you cannot hide from yourself. We hide from ourselves in many ways, such as always working and never spending a quiet moment by ourselves, always running away from self and reality, always having to do something, listening to our iPads and watching television. In addition, some of us are always on the computer, with no time to think about what the important things are in life, why we are here and where we are all heading.

Through His unbounded favour, the Eternal, our Creator, gave us a brain with billions of cells so that we can think, create and, the greatest gift of all, before the Eternal Father set up the foundation of the universe, ordained that mankind must have the freedom to choose. With that said, the greatest battle on this planet is for the mind. Remember that your Creator, the Lord, gave you and I the privilege to make our own choices, so we have to take our pick. Your Creator respects whatever choice you make, good or bad, but in His boundless love, the Eternal encourages us to choose life, so each one of us has the right and privilege to choose the way we live. We should, however, never forget that there are consequences to every choice we make, and we are our brain, which is in control of our body. Our thoughts and emotions, therefore, apprehend this fact, and the most urgent need today, at this very moment, is for each and every one of us to study and observe our own mind carefully. I cannot think of a more important subject matter.

If you take a moment to pause and look around, everything you see first has its genesis or beginning in the mind, the brain, and every concept and every idea first starts in the mind. Is it a small thing that we should neglect the development of our minds and leave it for others to do, and leave our most precious asset, our brains, to be violated, damaged and washed? To do such a thing is to violate your own person. As I have said before, an intelligent person, one who is humble in spirit, always listens to everyone. They know that even the disabled have their story to tell, so listen to your doctor, your preacher and your teacher, and after listening to everyone, it is now your special moment to think for yourself. The next step is to utilize and synthesize the information for yourself, by thinking for yourself and not waiting for someone to spoon feed you.

Because of the knowledge you now acquire because of your own self-analysis, it can be said of yourself that you know a thing or two. If you proclaim that you have knowledge about a particular subject, what you are announcing to the world is that the information you acquired has become your personal knowledge. Why? Because your own brain and frame of reference, your own logic and realization, through reasoning, concludes that the information is correct in your own mind. This process must filter all information.

## Be Childlike, Not Childish, and Know Yourself

If anyone tells you that observing your own mind is easy, they are lying to you. To think for yourself is far from easy. Additionally, to work for a living for your family is not easy, but we all do work, with pleasure. Why? Because of the benefits we receive: We exercise our body and mind, and we are able to take care of our family, and that is important. If thinking about and observing your thoughts was so easy, then more of us would be thinking for ourselves; instead, we let other people think for us.

Be childlike, not childish. As Yeshua the Christ stated, if anyone—and that means anyone—wants to have redemption or life forever, they have to be childlike. This means we should be having the attitude of a child—forgiving, not holding grudges, and humility to not take everything personally—and with this kind of attitude, the brain is more still and you can think better. Remember the Eternal: Speak, be still and know that I am. Be still in your mind and say goodbye to fear. When you are full of fear, you die many times; that is how destructive fear is. You can choose to use your mind or lose it; anything you do not use, you lose. Your natural intuitive self will not condemn you, but it will embrace you. As it is written, "Man, know thyself, and to thine self be true."

By knowing your inner self, you will know God, and because of the correct knowledge of self, you start to see things in a new light; you start to see yourself and God in every other human. Each to all and all to one another. We belong to each other; this is what is called a divine arrangement or oneness—one humanity. All the wars you see on this planet are because of separation; we do not see ourselves in each other, and then we start to compare ourselves with each other, and then the war starts. Our true self will teach us that we are all one, and this concept of oneness will start first in the family and then spread out to the community, then to the nation, then to humanity.

Self-realization will help you to discover your true purpose in life, which is to receive your redemption; that is to say, each one of us was born or created with an awesome purpose endowed by the Creator himself, and that purpose is to develop true character. Character is your thoughts, emotions and moral imagination, and we are not talking about reputation, which is what men think of us through their egotistical self. Furthermore, character has to be developed through free volition and free thought, and character can be created.

We have to choose to do the right thing and, as human beings, we have to learn that there is only one sovereign in the universe, the Eternal. He must be held in the highest reverence, and it is also important to apprehend that the Eternal most holy is not a man and He cannot lie, and we as humans must be careful to follow His instructions. He set before us two paths: life or death. Although we have free thought, He the Lord did not just say to take your pick. He encouraged us to choose life.

We all know that each choice we make as an individual or collectively does have consequences, and we need to stop this madness of blaming God for everything that goes wrong in our lives. Additionally, we need to take full responsibility for our actions, period. We have to blame ourselves for the problems we get ourselves into, even if someone else contributes to that problem. Bear in mind also that we are the ones who ultimately choose by our own will, to follow our desires of greed and our ultra ego.

The days of blaming the evil one, Satan, are long gone, and the more a person takes responsibility for his actions, the stronger he gets mentally and spiritually, and he stops blaming others for his behavior. Taking responsibility is a sign of maturity and being true to self. It is a sign of character.

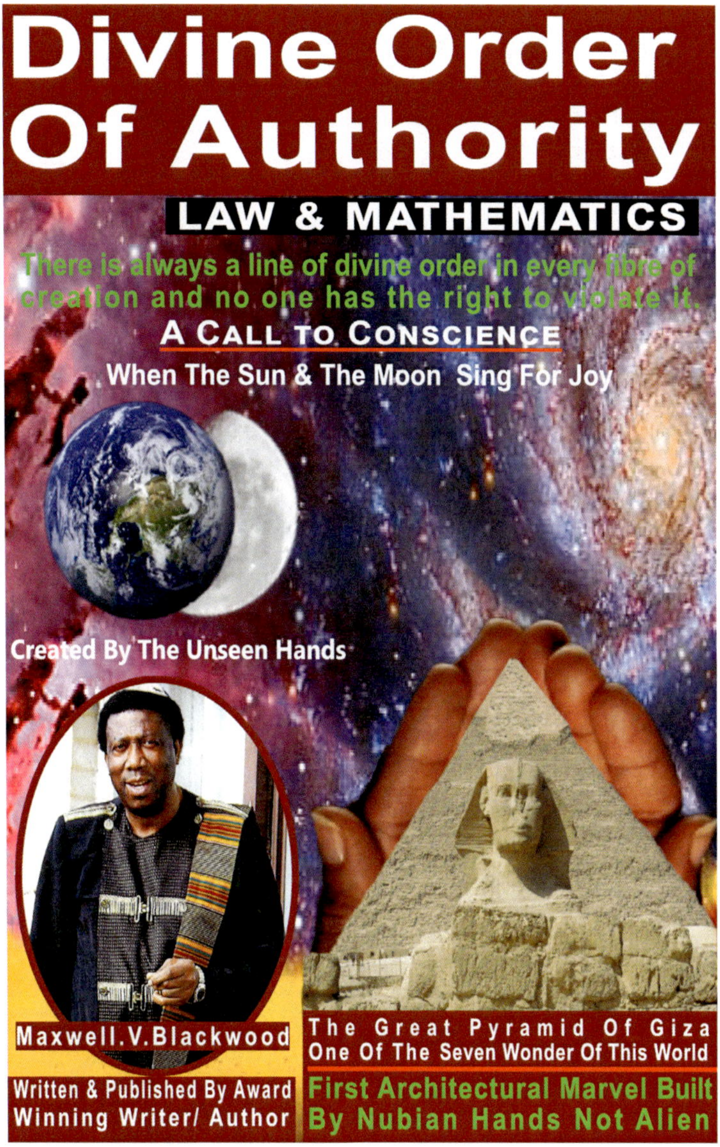


*Initial idea for the design of the book cover.*

*Seen here (from left to right) is Ben Johnson, one of the fastest men in the world and gold Olympian during his youth, shaking hands with Maxwell Blackwood at the Black Diamond Art Gallery, on Eglinton Ave West.*

*Seen here is one of my (Maxwell) favourite nieces, attorney at law, Janet Blackwood. She is always with my brother and taking care of him.*

*Seen here (from left to right) is president of NCU,
Dr. Edward Lincoln, who was congratulating Mr. Guy Steers
for receiving his honorary doctorate in business.*

*Seen here is a tranquil setting showing a few things in nature; however, the main thing to note is that it illustrates the forces of darkness that produce light.*

*Two is better than one.*

*Like water, love will find its way.*

*Seen here (from left to right) is Judge Donald McLeod, sharing a light moment with Maxwell. This site is the chambers where judge McLeod judicates at the Brampton Court.*

*The Moringa plant is one of the original healing plants used in Africa.*

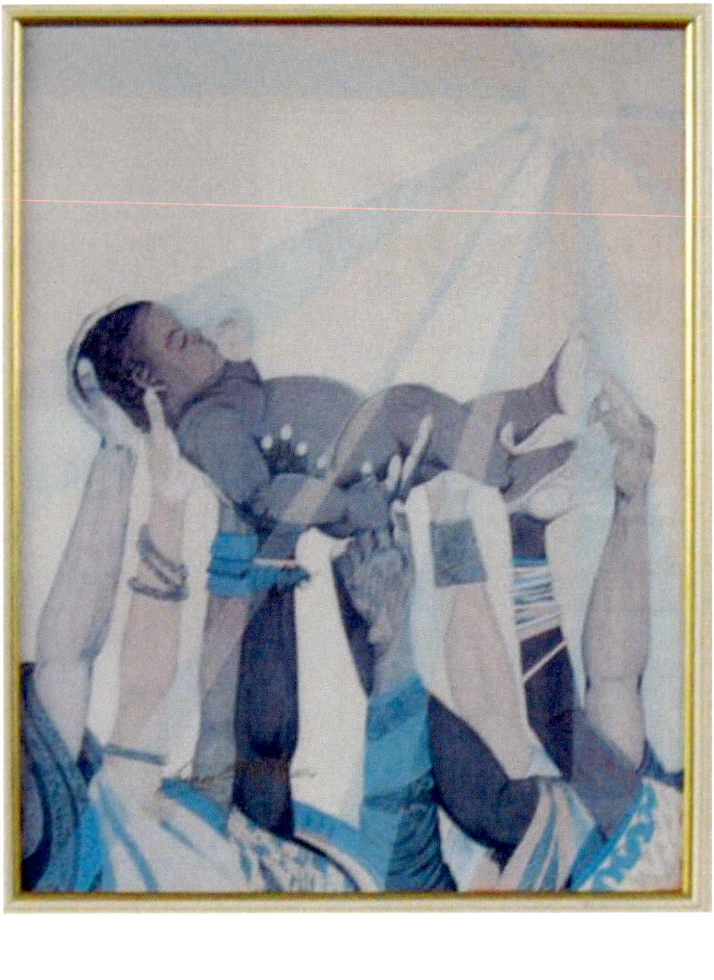

*This picture is very symbolic. Culturally, regardless of race or skin colour, blessings are asked on all our children. We are asking the Creator to instill the culture into the memory banks of our children.*

*"Horses aren't a hobby you pick up and sit back down. They are a love that lasts a lifetime."*

*Seen here (from left to right) are Maxwell and his first born son, Andrew Maxwell.*

*Seen here (front left to right) are Maxwell and Northern Caribbean University president, Dr. Lincoln, showing off one of the coveted trophies of the institution's long list of wins.*

*One of the pieces from the Black Diamond Art Gallery.*

*An African sculpture of a musician,*
*which is a piece from the Black Diamond Art Gallery.*

*Painting of 2 Nubian princesses.*
*This is a piece from the Black Diamond Art Gallery.*

*Seen here is Cathlena Cleghorn, one of my mothers from Cuba. Sis Joyce Hall, in Toronto, Canada, is another one of my mothers. They are spiritual mothers in Israel. I have several mothers, spiritually speaking.*

*Another piece from the gallery,
showing the forces of darkness that produce light.*

*Like water, love will always find its way.*

*I think I will never see a poem as lovely as a tree.*

*Castle of a shepherd, which is a piece that is at my residence.*

*A picture depicting the humility of power.*

*Seen here (from left to right) are Mr. Winston Larose and Maxwell. Mr. Larose was congratulated for receiving his honorary doctorate for the humanities, from the Northern Caribbean University.*

*Seen here is Maxwell's young family: wife, Norma Lewis-Blackwood, and children, Andrew, Valrie, and David. "A mother is she who can take the place of all others but whose place no one else can take."*
*– Cardinal Mermillod*

# World Wonder

## Paga Crocodile Pond

Paga is noted for its sacred pond, which is a sanctuary for crocodiles. The crocodiles are said to be totems for the people of Kassena, who reside in Paga and the surrounding communities. It is believed that each native of Paga has a corresponding crocodi representing each person's soul. Local tradition has it that there have been actual instances when deaths of important personalities the community coincided with that of some crocodiles. The reptiles are normally enticed out of the pond by the whistling of the caretaker and the brandishing of a fowl, which the crocodiles quickly snatch with their snouts. If you are courageous, you can sit on, or hold the beast's tail for a good camera pose. The caretaker charges a fee for the fowl and basic interpretation

60 World Wonder

*In the new order, the lion and the lamb and the crocodile will dwell in harmony, and a little child will lead them.*

**Nancy Angeline First Year**

Happy Birthday Nancy Angeline on your first year on this planet earth, hope you enjoy many more years, seen here with her older sister Gaby, still living in beautiful Cuba enjoying the sun shine, grand daughter of Magalis Benito.

*Even for the sparrow, the most merciful One*
*provides blackberries in the snow.*
*Will the Creator not provide even more for you?*
*Think about it.*

# Youth Poet

## Shhhhhh

*Celestina malkuth Francis*

A letter to you from God

Let peace reign,

And overshadow all terrains.

Whether white, black or yellow fellow flowers,

We all bloom.

Love is the one thing that nourishes our roots.

Our core pigment,

And keeps it bright.

Don't let it go dull, or white,

Nor black face the black fellow flower,

But face back the black flower with your own colour.

Be you.

White, Black or blue.

Blossom pretty flower

I love you.

**Celestina malkuth Francis**

Email: celestinafrancis35@gmail.com
Website www.scarletcrystal.com
IG:scarlet_crystal___
YT: Heavenly Poetry

*Say hello to one of the most hardworking and organized students ever, Celistina Francis. Her aspiration is to become a physician (doctor). She is a poet and an artist, and here we are sharing one of her poems with you.*

*Seen here (from left to right) are Maxwell and Dr. Noel Fraser, former president of the West Jamaica Conference of Seventh Day Adventist. Dr. Fraser is the man with the priceless smile. We ran into each other at the front of the fellowship hall of the chapel that we were visiting at NCU. As a young pastor in the conference, I vividly remember Pastor Fraser and my father working very closely together in the church district, in St. Elizabeth and St. James in Jamaica. My father used to be a leader and elder in several of the churches within the area. Two of the churches I recall attending as a young lad are Huntly Castle and Line Gate SDA church.*

*Young Pastor Peyton was also working in the district of these two churches. He migrated to Toronto, Canada, and worked here in pastoral positions, and now he is retired.*

*I would like to invoke the names of a few of the leaders at Line Gate Church:*
**Daisy Duncan, treasurer*
**Bro. Williams, elder*
**Jephet Bowen (He gave land to build churches.)*

*At the Huntley Castle Church, I want to invoke these names:*
**Bro. Kerr and his wife Sis Tat*
**Bro. Burnitt (close friend of my father) and Sis Nen, just to name a few.*

*You might ask why I call these names. By calling their names, they live again. As you know, when someone is more senior in Jamaica, we refer to them as brother this and sister that. From an Afrocentric standpoint, we always speak of elders as uncle and aunt. Children nowadays lose respect for elders, and it is our responsibility as parents to teach them the right thing.*

## The One God Concept Is a Nubian Concept (African Concept)

One of the divine orders of the Lord is the "Isness," or being of things, that the Eternal most holy is the only sovereign One in the entire universe; that is, all creation, man or angels, live and move and have their being by and from the Eternal. That is to say, the properties that hold things together would disperse the law of chemistry, and would not work without divine order.

Let us back up for a moment. What I was trying to say is that in fact, the Eternal alone is sovereign, and that He alone deserves homage and must be held in the highest reverence, and His instructions must be obeyed with meticulous care. Why so, you may ask? Because He alone is the One who cares. *Hear O Israel: Your Lord thy God is one; you cannot have two Gods*. Anything else would be a rival of the Eternal, who has no competition. The one God concept brings all humanity together as one. It remains written that the Word of the Lord your God, the Eternal, is one.

The concept of the one God, like all aspects of the Eternal's character, has to be understood in its correct context. It has been stated before that those of us who want to know the Lord the Eternal, in a true way, have to know His order. It is important to be reminded why this book is entitled *Divine Order of Authority*; that is, anything we as human beings claim that we know, we have to study and apprehend that subject based on its nature and the order of that thing.

The one God concept, understood correctly, can help us to appreciate and understand the nature and order of the Eternal. The Eternal knows it would be impossible to have more than one God, and the one God concept creates unity and oneness in the universe. Can you imagine us human beings all having our own god? You know how humans can be egotistical, full of pride or vain. We all would be bragging that our god is better than the other person's god. We would have more wars than we do today, and that is why I trust in the divine wisdom of the Eternal, who established the one god.

Millions of women, children and men all lift up their eyes to the one God. Nothing about the divine God is simple; therefore, we use our minds, human concepts and ideas to know about God.

Look at our world today—the war, the fighting—do you ever ask why all these things are happening? There are many reasons for the mayhem, but the main reason is man being self-absorbed or egotistical, and seeing each other as strangers. The one God concept helps us to see ourselves in each other, so there will be no strangers but one humanity, meaning each to all and all to one another. We belong to each other; this is the "Isness" of the divine order. When we start seeing God and ourselves in each other, there will be no strangers, to them or to us, and then war will be over. Then and only then will we as part of mankind, start to evolve into becoming true human beings.

Have you ever thought about what it means to be a true human being? Take a moment and think about that; it's not because you have two hands and two feet—that does not make you a human. On the contrary, truly to be a real human, you have to be filled with compassion and intelligence. So if you and I would like to stop the madness on planet Earth today, it is imperative that we have the correct knowledge of the one God. This oneness of all humanity, the oneness of the universe, is a divine order; and all divine orders are designed to bring love, balance, harmony and peace. Remember, divine order means law.

The Eternal alone can make laws, while man can only make rules and regulations, and they change from time to time, but the Eternal's laws are unchangeable, timeless, immutable and boundless. All God's laws are designed for our happiness, and they emanate from agape love, and the Eternal uses all His divine laws as a medium to carry out His master plan. The laws of physics, gravity and chemistry, and the moral principles that remain written in the holy volume, are all laws for our good, and to maintain harmony in our universe. Can you just imagine an individual or group who is advocating that these divine orders or laws are no longer applicable today? This type of reasoning is what is called real insanity or madness, and as stated before, God's laws are for our good. Man cannot make or change divine order or law, because the eternal decree that man must have freedom of choice and free thought, was made before the foundation of the world. This, therefore, means that all of us can choose to disobey God's will but not without facing the real consequences of our actions.

Let us continue to share ideas on this all important concept, the one God. Many people think that because they read in the holy book about different personages and personalities of God, that it has to mean that there is more than one God. Let us first agree on one thing: that human knowledge on any subject matter about God is always very limited. Please remember that you are talking about the most holy eternal God, who cannot be found by searching. You just have to be still and know that the words "I Am," "Isness," and "God" are not singular but actually plural; that is to say, more than one personage in the God family but only God. One of the ways we can know about God is to use human concepts and ideas. For example, my family name is Blackwood, and I have many members or individuals who are in my family, but only in one Blackwood family. Likewise, the eternal God family has more than one personality in that God family; however, only one God, the One who created heaven and the Earth. Do you know of anyone else who can create heaven and Earth? Let me know when you find out the answer.

In the Godhead or the God family, the expression triune God—that is to say, there are three personages—are all God in their own right, and all are one among these three that are acting in different roles in the divine master plan for the redemption of all humanity. I am using human concepts and ideas to define the undefinable; however, natural human concepts and ideas are limited at best to describe divinity. Even as I struggle to explain these great truths, you need to know, as readers, that I am just using human language to give you an idea of my understanding of the subject matter about the Godhead, the god family.

As I have said, I am just sharing my thoughts and ideas about the subject. Therefore, as readers, you have to use your own minds, use logic and realize with a divine mind to understand the issues for yourself.

## Train Your Mind (Brain), Change Your Life

No one can think for you, and if you used to let people think for you, that time has long gone. In fact, this is a new reality, and you have to shift the burden to think for yourself, no more to be spoon-fed. You are your own universe, with a mind of staggering potential, and it is time to dive into the sea of knowledge, to do business in deep waters of self-discovery, self-knowledge and self-analysis. We like others to think for us because we like the easy way out, and basically, we are too lazy to think. In other words, we are evading the responsibility of our actions and choices. For so long, we enjoyed having our professor, teacher, preacher and our social experts package or wrap everything, and spoon-feed us about matters of importance, without thinking for ourselves.

I cannot overemphasize how important it is that as intelligent persons, we should listen to everyone, including the philosopher, but always reserve the right to think and analyze things for yourself. Each one of us is our own individual, having different frames of references. We can only know God through human concepts and ideas, as we are living in a parallel universe, a world of duality, a world of contrast—like having sunshine and rain, you have darkness and light and you have female and male. God is the primum mobile, but we have seen through our minds' eyes, the first begotten of the Father, the Christ, as one and the same, but as a contrast so that we can appreciate the role of the Father.

We always have to remember several things and synthesize in our brain that we are using human concepts to decipher things of divine nature. Human concept is always limited to define infinity, but human concept is what we have to help us to have a better appreciation of the divine plan and duality at work, human and divine. Additionally, human concepts and ideas through language are the medium we use to understand God and His master plan, notwithstanding the limitation of our concepts, imagination and ideas.

If we apply our billions of brain cells, with our body cells, we can even levitate; that is to say, we could fly not only mentally but physically, and if your brain is trained well, then your mind can gain altitude and emanation. Once your thoughts are in flight, for you to fly that thing, your thoughts, or aircraft, have to develop lots of speed and heat. Once you have the right amount of speed, then you will get the right amount of heat. Speed and heat change the chemistry in your body or your brain, and once your chemistry changes, everything changes, in image and colour; that is where the concept of your ultrasound comes from.

I have to back up a little just to emphasize the importance of *training your own brain*. If we are using human concept, ideas and imagination to know God and His master plan of redemption, we have to train our minds to understand human concepts and ideas in their correct context historically. This is critical for you to have the proper frame of reference so that you are well informed, as your life depends on knowing the truth.

Morality, in our imagination, is our greatest need at this moment in time, to use culture, concept, ideas and human language as a frame of reference to apprehend the Eternal's purpose for our lives. It will not only take moral imagination but also your brain and body cells' power to discipline yourself. With that alter ego, greed and selfish nature, we humans are funny; we think that someone out there is our enemy, but the real enemy is ourselves. When you think of ego, self, greed and false pride, are you ready to deal with this dangerous enemy, the self? To deal with yourself, you have to first know yourself, and you also have to be true to yourself.

One of the greatest axioms that remains in the permitted text, says: *"Man, know thyself, and to thine self be true."* By knowing *yourself*, your own universe, you will know God, because self-knowledge is the highest form of knowledge. Self-discovery of your higher self is when you can understand the word of the Eternal as it remains written in the holy book. "I, the Lord, created mankind in my own image, male and female. I ask this question again: Do you know what it means to be a human being? Do not answer; just be still and think, as not every question has an answer. Sometimes the answer is in the question, for the question is the key.

Any person who is always looking for answers to all their questions, is not fully integrated, knowledge wise. One of the concepts of human relationships the Eternal chose to use, to make plain His divine plan of redemption for humanity, is the father and son relationship. The concept of using human experiences to make plain divine truth, has to be studied with much care. All of our human experiences are earthbound. Just think for a moment if someone else from another planet suddenly appeared and spoke to you in their tongue or language—as a human, you would not understand the language. That is the point I am trying to make. If the eternal God speaks to us humans in a heavenly language, we would have difficulty understanding, so the good Lord in His wisdom uses human concepts and ideas in language, to get across to us His message of love. By using a human relationship, we know the Father and Son concept.

In the holy volume, it remains written: "For God so loved the world that he gave His only begotten son." You know the rest of that verse. It remains also written in the Book of Psalms, with the sublime most holy eternal God speaking, "I will make a decree today that you will become my son." Before the foundation of the universe was created, the eternal Godhead already had a master plan to redeem humanity, in case mankind, by his own choice, rejected His government. The Eternal was not taken by surprise. In fact, the Holy One possesses all knowledge of past, present and future, so He, the Eternal, knows why the Godhead fashioned man from the black clay. He knows that the man He was making could choose to disobey His rule, but the Lord most merciful decreed that man must make his or her own choice.

If mankind chooses to rebel against his Creator, the Eternal would be justified if He permitted man to go on his rebellious path and lose his redemption for which he was created, so the Eternal so loved us that He made a way out. Remember, He is the way maker, and because God cannot have a son in the context of divinity, it was decreed by the eternal Godhead, in that God family. Remember, the word "God" is not singular, so each member of the triune God family plays different roles. One plays the Father God, the other the Son of God, and the other the Spirit of God role.

*Here O Israel: your Lord your God is one*—not one in personality but in purpose, to save humanity from themselves. So the father and son relationship was established as a divine order. For God so loved that He gave His son, and so loved the world that He gave himself. I gave up my own life, and a body was prepared for me. It remains written that the spirit of the living God gave himself; everything was given by the eternal Godhead for our great salvation. The question is, what are you going to do if you reject so great a salvation? "Be still and know that I am."

# Human Concepts and Ideas Create the Cosmos (or the World)

We humans have an idea what it means to lose a child. The blessed One has given us humans the privilege to reproduce ourselves through our children. We also continue to live through our children, so now we see that the father and son relationship was established and decreed by the triune eternal God to give man a "bird's eye view" into His master plan, the redemption story. God uses ordinary people, language, words, human concepts and ideas to convey His love and salvation to us. The Eternal is fully aware that using human concepts and ideas, with their human limitations at best, has the potential of misunderstanding. So the question before us is, can human concepts and ideas give us a balanced understanding of the eternal plan for us? I would answer yes and no.

Remember, when we started this little dialogue, we expressed the ideas generally; the Eternal does things in duality. This means part human and part divine. When a human's good intention is coupled with a desire to please the Lord, then that said desire pleases the Lord. Even if, at the moment, we are not actually doing His will, He the Holy One knows how weak and fragile our memory is—the "Isness" of things. However, this is not an excuse, and the Eternal knows our nature as He created us.

Let us back up a little; we are saying that if man cultivates the right attitude, a humble spirit, a desire to please the Lord, when man and divine come together, there is nothing that we cannot accomplish. If I know us humans well, we always want to follow our own ways. Let us, as of today, follow our master teacher, Christ. Now that we have expressed our human view about our concepts and ideas, with its limitations at best, we now know that whatever we know about God, comes from our human concepts and ideas. We need to confess and acknowledge that there is a lot we do not yet know about our great and loving eternal God. But we do not have to despair. We just have to humble ourselves, stop pretending to be experts on everything and accept that man knows nothing. The person who comes to the most merciful eternal God and admits they know nothing, will have the master Christ teach them everything they need to know about His will.

With that in mind, let us do a little summary. In our little talk, we came to realize that as part of the family of man, to know about God, we use human concepts, ideas, words and language. When we speak of God in this context, we are making reference to the divine. You and I should know that mere human concepts, ideas, words and language cannot fully define the Eternal. For anyone to understand a subject matter properly, you have to speak in that person's language; therefore, the Eternal, in His divine wisdom, speaks to us in our human language, not in an angelic language.

Human concepts and languages at best have their limitations. To define divine wisdom, please remember the duality in life, divine and human. The human aspect, in this context, is "Isness." In regard to His concept, language, divine input and divine inspiration, through the thoughts and concepts of humans, there is always the possibility of error when using human concept and language to define divine wisdom. But whenever humans connect intent and their desire to obey the divine will, the outcome is never in doubt. It is an excellent outcome—human and divine working together equals redemption.

As humans, we must always remember that God is not a man, so every word that he speaks is absolute truth, even if we humans do not understand everything. We must express the attitude of obedience to His divine will, which pleases the Lord. Like the song says, words without love are words without meaning, and there is some truth to this expression. Words or language that are not saturated with the love of God, are really words without meaning.

As humans, we use words and language to communicate with each other, and we generally think that this is the only way to communicate. The fact is, there are other forms of expression or communication that are beyond words. Whenever you look at a beautiful flower in admiration, do you hear any words or language from that flower? But that flower is talking to you in a loud voice. Are you listening? So now we learn that communication is not just verbal but also nonverbal, meaning words and language are not the only ways to communicate.

There are other higher forms of expression that have nothing to do with word or language for that matter, so let us back up a little and synthesize our thoughts for a moment. We come to understand that words, language, concepts and ideas are human instruments that we use to know about God, who is divine. From a human standpoint, human concepts are limited to give a clear view of the eternal plan, but we have to use what we have, like the Eternal said to His noble prophet Moses. What is "Isness?" You have it in your hand, so use it. We have human concepts and ideas to learn about God, so let us use them to the best of our ability and stop complaining when word, language, human concepts and ideas fail to give us a clear apprehension of the master plan and our redemption.

It remains written in the holy book that when we use what we have, to the best of our ability, and educate ourselves, the very spirit of the living God will bring back to our memory things we have learned over time. Through our culture and concept, the spirit of the Eternal will open our minds to understanding, even though we are using human concept—and we all agree it is very limited—to pierce into the divine mind. Nevertheless, the Eternal, in His boundless favour, gives us all a super brain, and if trained well, it will help us to apprehend, conceptualize, realize, visualize and, the greatest of all, inspire. That is when our minds are breathed upon in a special kind of way, by the most Holy One. It is impossible for human words and language to give the full picture of the eternal plan for man, but when human and divine inspiration come together, then we will see real miracles, and that is the "Isness." We influence each other in a positive way, for the good of many.

We established that using words and language is not the only way to communicate; there are other higher forms of communication. Have you ever stood back in stillness and looked at the mighty ocean or sea? Did you hear the ocean speaking to you at that moment without a word? Did you hear that? We use words every day. Many people believe that because they are using a word, it means they know what that word means. Using a word and actually knowing the meaning of it are two different things. Let's take a look at the word "God." First, you have to know that the word "God" is not God as in this context—we are talking about divinity.

Words are like a sign post, which is usually pointing you to somewhere or something. Furthermore words sometimes do not define themselves, and you have to search under, above and around the world. Which group of people speak those words? In what context and text were those words spoken? Which land and culture? These are all vital things you need to know in order to have a correct knowledge of words and their meaning. The eternal God is called by many names, but there is only one God. Because words are limited, this one God is called by many different names. Our loving Father is the same, for your God and my God are one, so we do not have to fight each other.

We have the same Father God and are all one humanity, made from the same cloth or dust of the Earth. We all have to see ourselves in each other, and the moment we stop the separation and start to see ourselves in each other, the evolution would have already begun. A mind shift to become a true human being, a real human, is the "Isness," meaning one who possesses compassion and intelligence. Do you really know what it means to be a real human being? We have to evolve from just being a part of mankind, to being a real human being.

We have been talking for a little while now, about words, language, human concept and ideas, and we are proposing to you that we use the human concept to know about God and His master plan for our lives. Moreover, we also emphasized that words and language are not enough and are very limited to define divinity. It is written in the holy volume that eyes have not seen, ears have not heard and neither has it even entered into the heart and mind of man, what God has provided for us.

Human words and language can just give us a bird's eye view into God's master plan, and this is why it is very important for each and every one of us to guard and develop our own minds. This is vital so that the divine One can inspire and breathe into our minds through the indwelling Christ, the very spirit of the living eternal God. It is then and only then that we can really see the whole picture, the big picture of the real purpose of your birth, with true self-discovery and the correct concept of self, coupled with knowledge of your true purpose in life. With this intelligence and wisdom, the intelligence of the power of intellect, you will get up each day with zest and a spring in your step, and never again will you give in to mad thoughts that you want to kill yourself and so on. Now you will look forward to every day with trust and gladness, and that makes such a difference in life—not believing but knowing. Be still and know. Know what? Know God, and know yourself. By discovering yourself, you know God simultaneously.

Let us back up one more time. Words and language are like a sign post; they are pointing you to somewhere or to something. You have to study letters in anagrammatic writing. Certain letters can be used as a word, like the letters e, h, o or r, and sometimes two letters can be used as a word. You can use two letters for the word "mister," for example, as the word itself (Mr.), and you can use three letters for the word mistress (Mrs.). I am just trying to stress the point that we must study words, letters, language and numbers. Some numbers are equivalent to certain letters, and vice versa. Most of us did not study linguistics; that is to study language as a subject matter. We humans make use of language to communicate with each other. That means we must know all we can know about words, language and numbers, so that we can have choices when we communicate with each other. As we stated before, words and language are like a signpost pointing to something. We have to dig beneath, on top and around that word, that letter or that number, and try to find out what they mean. We have to stop laziness and start to study and think for ourselves, as our lives depend on it. Sometimes words or language do not fully describe the intended object.

Let us look at the word "love." The word "love" is not love. We use the word "love" every day, and we are still hurting each other. We always have to remember that just because we use a word, it doesn't necessarily mean that we know the meaning of such a word. To say you know a thing, is to have correct knowledge of that thing, what it can do and what it cannot do. Your family, brain, mind—who is in control? You are in control. *The greatest battle that still goes on at this very moment in time is the "Isness." For your mind, do not let them.*

# Guard Your Mind, Mind Your Mind or Mind Your Own Business

It remains written by the wisest man that ever lived; and in talking about the mind, he stated to all of us that we must guard the heart and mind with all diligence. This is critical, as your life depends on it, and the battle for the mind is on. Everywhere you look, someone is asking for your attention. There are so many choices, and everybody wants to control your mind. *I will say it again: Do not let them.* You are the only one who has the right to control and develop your own mind. Not even the eternal God, who created you, has any interest in controlling your mind, and that is why He created all of us with free thought and free choices. I do not understand the obsession of men who want to control the lives and minds of other men. Truly, this is insanity in its highest form.

The eternal God made all things beautiful and free, and every fibre of His creation was meant to be free, so what and who is man that he wants to control every insight, in his mad state. I personally think that man has overrated himself.

If we humans accept God's master plan for our lives, then we are forced for good, with mind staggering potential. We have the free choice also to reject the eternal master plan for our lives. Think for a moment; do you really know what and who you are rejecting? The killings in our lives and the world at large today, are a direct result of rejecting the eternal master plan for our lives. For every action, there is an opposite reaction, and we reap what we sow. These living principles or laws cannot be violated or go unpunished. God is not the one who is punishing us; in our egotistical and selfish state, we are the ones who are destroying ourselves. One of the greatest words in the English language is the word "come." "Come let us reason together," said the Lord of host. Just imagine for a moment that the Holy One would like to have a little talk with you and me. Anytime someone wants to talk with you, it is out of respect, and it is one who values your presence. Come, come, come! You do not have to bear your pain alone. Oh, what needless pain we bear. Come, there is a balm in Gilead that can heal your sin-sick soul, so you do not have to die. We are created with free thought, and we have the power to choose to live.

The expression, "There is a balm in Gilead to heal a sin-sick soul," is making reference to Christ, who is the only true healer. There is no one else who died for you except Christ, and it is by His stripes that we are all healed. The concept or expression, *"There is a balm in Gilead,"* has direct connection to this place in Africa and is known for its healing herbs. Even now, people use those medicinal plants to aid the body to heal itself. The body has the power to heal itself, so the next time you feel any pain, your body is trying to talk to you and tell you to pay attention. The question is, truthfully, will you listen? Most of us, if not all, do not listen when our bodies talk, and tend to be more in tune with our cars than our bodies. What insanity! Let us all heed the call and start listening to our minds, souls and bodies.

# The Family, the Foundation of Humanity and Society

Church, state, title—what are their roles and responsibilities? It is important to note that whenever you are studying any subject matter, you should always look at it from a cause and effect standpoint and from its beginning. By doing so, you will have a better understanding about the subject matter. In this case, we are discussing the subject, the role of the church and the role of the state. Before there was any church or state, there was the family, so the family was the first community. From the family comes the church and then the state, so it is becoming clearer that for us to have a good society, we first must have a well-cultivated and organized family unit.

The supreme role of the church and the state, first and foremost, is to protect the citizenry and create a safe environment so that citizens with free thought can develop their full potential. Citizens have sovereignty; that is, they are the ones who have legitimacy—with the people lies the power. Under any form of government—it does not matter if it is the church, the parliamentary democracy or autocracy rule (like the queen of England)—citizens are always in charge. This simply means, where the seat of power lies with the people, citizens are responsible, to a lesser or a greater degree, for the abuse of power by their government. I say that because we are the ones that vote them into power, time and time again, notwithstanding the lies they keep feeding us. I started writing this book in 2007, and I was expressing the view that it is past the time for citizens of the world, all over this planet, to rise and take back the government. The real power lies with the citizens, not with big businesses/organizations, the elites or the government. Citizens need to rediscover their responsibility. I have never seen this type of insanity where the government uses state property as if it were their personal belongings.

Many people are ignorant to the fact that the state belongs to the citizens, and the law emanates from the people, which means people are the ones who make laws, while the government may be the one who breaks these laws. Indeed, the law really comes from the people. I live in Canada and know Ottawa is the capital; however, it would not be feasible or practical for all the citizens of Canada to march to Ottawa to administer the country. That action would result in utter chaos, the opposite of which is balance that produces harmony; and as citizens, we need balance and harmony to function. That said, citizens must choose qualified representatives in all aspects of government that represent the interest and the good of the many, instead of the interest of some narrow-minded politicians and their party polities that are pregnant with self-interest. The time for party politics has long gone. Now is the time for a call to conscience and for all governments of the world to work for the interest and good of the many.

What is the role and responsibility of the church in the world and the community? It should be like the government of a country, which must exist for the citizens' welfare and protection. When this fact ceases to be the focal point of the church or the government, then those entities lose their purpose to exist and their legitimacy. The church's role is even more important than the government, in that the church is entrusted with the souls of men/mankind; that is, the "Isness." In other words, the church deals with the here and now and the hereafter, and when it negates the communal roles and care for the dying, people will lose their salvation for which they were created. The dying in this case implies to those who are living in poverty.

Without a doubt, this is an awesome, mind-stretching responsibility. Glory and inspiration tells us that of all the institutions on this planet Earth, the eternal God placed his highest regard on His church. Apprehending this fact, how can the church abort their God-given responsibility?

If you know anything about the first century church—and remember, when I speak of the church, I am not talking about a building—the word "church," in its original context, means the call out ones. Call out from where and what? Call from this world's system of things, deception, misinformation, crime against humanity, abuse against children, women and the elderly, inhumanity of man to man, and slavery and captivity, just to name a few. These are the shame of mankind and are some of the things the church must be called out from. I am personally making a call to the church of the living eternal God, for us to recover our God-given purpose in our world today. The only reason or purpose for the church to exist is to nurture and empower its members, and every other thing we do must be designed to encourage the membership. This therefore means that if we build an edifice for the church to worship and fellowship therein, and build schools and  hospitals, I know we need to build community centres for our children and youth.

We need to build more community centres than churches, and bear in mind that our children and youth are the future of the church. If we do not educate our children in all the arts, and nurture them, you know the kind of future we will have. We have lost more than one generation already, so can we afford to lose another? I hope we get the point. Whatever we are doing as a church community, building, school, hospital, place of worship, or organization structure, all these are important in their correct context and have only one purpose, which is to serve the citizen's membership. If we fail as a church community to live out these ideals, to live and to serve our community, we would have aborted our real purpose to exist. I pray that heaven may help us all to rediscover our role in the world and to bring healing. To some extent, the church has failed to protect our children and our senior citizens.

Our children are our future and inheritance, and we continue to live through our children, as well as our elders who are our treasure, and our honorary citizens. In the African worldview, the elders are much respected. You see, the elders know the history and are like a walking library. There is no generation gap, because the young need the elders since they have the experience and the history to teach the young. On the other hand, the elders need the young, with their energy, veracity and imagination.

It is to our loss and our shame (humanity shame) when we do not teach our children to respect their elders. This is a divine order, to teach our children respect and honour. Anyone, including myself, that tries to make an excuse, is insane. Do you see the chaos in our society today? It has something to do with our negligence as adults, in not instilling correct discipline and respect in our children, period. I think, personally, the largest shame on humanity is the abuse of our children and elderly, the two most valuable groups in our society. Moreover, it is a crime against humanity when we permit children to starve to death in a world that has plenty of food; so much so that food corporations throw food away every day. This is a shame to humanity when all the children of the world truly belong to each and every one of us; we do not have to give birth to them to call them our own.

We are the world, and we are the people, so we are collectively responsible for the abuse of the children, to a lesser or greater degree. Therefore, when World Vision puts it on television that African babies are starving to death, this is not the shame of Africa but is the shame of humanity. Each and every one of us who are a part of mankind are complicit in some way for the suffering of our children. When we as adults violate our children sexually, what type of a crime is that? It is difficult to find words for that crime when we allow that type of abuse to take place. As abhorrent and repulsive as these crimes are, if we sit back in our easy chairs and do nothing to help and save the children, then we are a part of the problem. *An urgent call to action to all people of conscience, all over this planet, to rally together to save our children.*

Come and behold. As it has been said, those who wish to receive the boundless, unbounding blessing of the Eternal most gracious, need to know the order of the Eternal. Praise be He and exalted be His fame forever.

I was surprised as I started to study the importance of this subject (order), and that the people in the churches and schools do not realize that their success is dependent on them following order and proper protocol. The secular society in the business community and many of the secret societies, on the other hand, are very much aware of the fact that for them to achieve success in its true sense, they have to be in tune with and acknowledge and understand order and proper protocol. The businesses and their CEOs know that by following orders, they will be more successful, and they know that if they do not follow an order, there will be chaos, disorder, greed and violence. Any individual or nation who rejects order will never succeed. Any order that is followed will more likely lead to success in the secular or sacred society. The success is in the principle of the order.

We are living in an age, at this moment, where society/people believe they do not have to follow any order. In defying divine order, that is what I call real rebellion. I think the reason we behave this way is lack of self-knowledge.

## Youth Violence, Cause and Cost

The first thing to remember as a rule is that children live what they learn. If they learn self-respect at an early age in young adulthood, they will be respectful, not only to elders but to everyone. There is a reason for everything under the sun, and for laws that are in motion everywhere. For example, the law of attraction—this is where whatever you resist, will persist. What I am trying to say is that there is the law of cause and effect. Whatever we sow, we will reap. It is not bad luck. We adults produce a violent culture, and that is what we will reap, in our youth in particular.

Why are we surprised at how violent our children are? They learn it from us; and remember, all of us in duality are one collective consciousness, so all of us together as a society are responsible for this problem of violence in our children, and it will affect you. It does not matter if your children are directly involved. We are collectively a violent society. Have you looked at the television and listened to the radio? Take a read from the mainstream paper—guns, nudity and sex are everywhere. When you stand at the bus stop, take a look at the billboards—violence is everywhere. So why are you surprised at youth violence? We adults are the main causes; our children are merely our reflection.

I hope you do not think for a moment that I do not know about bad influence and peer pressure. I have three adult children, so I know this problem first hand, and I also know that we as parents play a very serious role in this problem of youth violence. We, as the parents, are the front line as far as our children are concerned, and when we let down our guard, then we leave our youth to be attacked by society, and all of us suffer. And I am not saying, as parents, that we have not tried, but that is not good enough. Children are worth fighting for with every ounce of blood in our body, is what I am trying to say; but as parents, a lot of us give up and become afraid of our children.

Once we abandon our parental role to others, such as the school, welfare, children's aide and all these agencies, then the result is violence. Greed generally turns into violence, then police involvement, and then, for sure, we may lose our children. This is the result when we do not invest in our children as parents first, and then as a society. We say our children are our future, but have you ever wondered, if we continue on this path, what kind of future awaits us? Do not be afraid to think about this.

The Ontario government asked two prominent parliamentarians to conduct a study into this issue of youth violence, some years ago. These persons were none other than Justice McMurtry MPP, and Alvin Curling, two veterans who should know something about this matter of youth violence. Alvin Curling was once a youth minister in the liberal government. I met Mr. Curling then and asked him, more than a decade ago, if he could recall that there are multi-facets or causes of this problem of youth violence. But one of the first things he could do as a youth minister and as a Nubian Moor himself (black), I thought at that time, would be to appreciate the problem better. Note, however, that genetically you cannot define a person by their colour. I hope you get my point.

# The Role of the Church, Community Policing and Government

Does the church, police and the government have a role to play in the community and the larger society? There are those of us who think that the government, church and the police organization have a role to play in society; however, it is clear that the majority of the citizens are not seeing their relevance in society.

## *The Church*

There are three entities that have a serious spiritual mandate, and these are none other than the church, police and government. These three exist for one purpose, and it is to serve the citizens in all capacities. Of all three, the church has the most vital role. It has both a spiritual and physical mandate; and yes, the church has a role to play in society and the world at large, but like the government and police, the church has abandoned its role. Instead of nurturing the people, they are building structures. I am not implying that structures do not have a role, but that is a sub-goal. People are the most important, so like the government and police, the church needs to rediscover its role and play it by standing up for the oppressed and speaking for them. Speak for those who cannot speak for themselves, set the captives free and advocate justice. Only the church can do that.

## *The Police*

True policing has to predicate from the principle of having a clear understanding of the constitutional rights of the citizens. So, essentially understanding their role and the role of the citizens is very critical.

All over the world, people are complaining about police brutality, whether in Canada, the USA, Jamaica or other countries, and the people believe that the police were never there for their protection and to serve them. We are not speaking based on the recent police abuse and murder of George Floyd and others; as police, abuse has been going on for a very long time.

The president of Northern Caribbean University (Dr. Lincoln), at a function some years ago (here in Canada), told us the role that the university plays in helping to train the constabulary force in Jamaica, and the big difference that training made. In his discourse here, he highlighted the training and the retraining in Jamaica. This training was about the well-being of the person (respect for their constitutional rights) who has that encounter with the police. We are now purporting that there is a role for policing, and that role has to be rediscovered, if it was ever discovered.

It is important to note what proper policing is, and to bear in mind that the people in the community are the ones who have information relating to what is happening within the community. Since this is so, the first role that the police should have is to have a good relationship with the people. The community will not bring information to the police when they don't trust the police; furthermore, if the police are only there when crimes are committed, it therefore means no proper policing was taking place in the first place.

So what has been happening now, in order for police to get information, is that they end up having to break the law to get intelligence or information. How is the law broken? The citizens' constitutional and chartered rights are violated when police collect the intelligence in the wrong way. Violation begins when the police or police agency starts carding, or in the case of New York, stopping and frisking the people. This practice is illegal.

Who actually has the right to stop and frisk the citizens? Unless there is a crime in progress, it doesn't necessarily mean the police have the right to speak to citizens. While the police have the right to speak to citizens only when a crime is in progress, the people also have the right to make a citizen's arrest.

As was said before, police have a role and, as discussed, proper policing is embedding the police into the community so that trust can be gained. When you have trust and respect for each party, the citizens of the community will be the ones that will be happy to give intelligence to the police, because the trust factor is established. Note that the police cannot be all things to the people, and it has to be a defined role.

Some examples of the roles can be controlling gang violence and organized crime; and in a more gentle, humane way, if a child is accidentally left at a daycare, the police can, in their capacity, go and help get the child back into the arms of his/her parents, where they belong. To help a senior who is in need, they may be of assistance to them when they are crossing the street, or when they have to fetch needed items from the store—those are examples of gentle, humane kindness that the police can show. These are commendable acts that any intelligent citizen would recommend for the police to practice. The police should not be sent to deal with mental health cases and non-violent family matters; and if you ask me, I don't think police should be put in such a position. Citizens' stomachs are literally sick to death that every time police are called to a scene, someone literally ends up being killed. That has to stop, and a new age of proper policing must emerge moving forward.

One of the things we also have to discuss is the proper way to address the police. When you address the police as "officer," that expression is incorrect. The correct way to address them is "constable" or "special constable." An officer is one who works for the government (which is owned by the people). Therefore, you can have an officer of the government; a barrister or solicitor is called an officer when they are in court. If you are part of the government in good standing, you can be called an officer also.

We should remember at all times that the citizen is sovereign; therefore, their constitutional rights must always be protected. So it is clear that police need to be retrained. The problem is great and truly has different causes, so training is not the only reason; the individual also has a role to play regarding their disposition. Most of all, they need to know what it means to be human. So again, we should agree that there is a role for police and proper policing.

### *The Government*

The next issue to address is the role of the government. Like the police, they have a role, but they are misguided (very misguided). The government, and also their very existence, is to serve the citizens. So, as we stated about the police, the government needs to rediscover its role. In actuality, when we talk about the government, the government is the citizen; therefore, the citizens are the ones who own the resources in the country (Canada). The water, tars and trees—everything in the country—belong to the citizens.

When the government mentions that they are giving billions here and there, the government is only the administrator over the people's affairs; however, the resources all belong to the people. We already know how the parliament democracy (so called) works, that the people are the ones who should choose their government, not big businesses. So the three levels of government exist to serve, whether you are in Queens Park, Ottawa or City Hall. Just like the police, they should remind themselves of who they actually work for, and they should be always mindful to govern (not rule) the people based on the constitutional and chartered rights.

The people's sovereignty must always be protected. The way I see it in regard to how the government behaves to their citizens, they overtax the citizens and waste the taxpayers' money. I think the government does have a role by having the citizens participate in issues that affect the family in particular. Either through election or referendum, the people should be the core of any functioning democracy.

The government also has a role to play, and there are certain things that they can do in the best interest of the citizens. When a large company, for example, poisons our drinking water, the citizens cannot take them to book. When pharmaceutical companies create bad drugs, the citizens cannot make things right with these large corporations. When predatory lenders, the banks and those who sell money overcharge the citizens with ridiculous interest, it's the role of the government to activate the Usury Act.

*In summary, the church, police and government have a role in society; however, they need to be realigned with the best interest of the people or citizens.*

# Black Sabbath

I know that many people reading this heading are immediately going to think about the musical group Black Sabbath; however, that has nothing to do with what I will be discussing.

The universe is founded on law and order, so the Eternal in His wisdom created law, which is order, so that His universe can operate in a harmonious way. In essence, the Eternal governs through His law.

One of His divine orders was to create time (what we call time), because in certain strata of the Universe, there is no time (timelessness). In creating time, the Eternal sectionalizes time, which is to say that He lays out time through a seven-day period, and He did that to give human beings a protocol to function or create a balance. In doing so, as He sectionalized time, He showed an example to us, as humans, that He himself took time off from that sectionalized period we call a week, and He rested (not that He was tired of course).

*He set an example as He gives us the instruction that we should follow Him; even though He cannot be tired (humans can get tired), He rested on the seventh day. Hence, we get the title Black Sabbath. The first two human beings who celebrated the Sabbath were created in the Garden of Eden, from black clay. Even today, we have that black clay in Iraq (which is part of Eden), which many use to make bricks.*

There were two original institutions created in the Garden of Eden, namely marriage and the Sabbath, but a lot of people, especially the so-called pastors, want to keep the marriage but not the Sabbath, which is dishonest. The fanatics will say God did away with the Sabbath; however, no such thing was done. The same Jesus (black Christ of Nazareth that people talk about) himself said the Sabbath was made for man, not man for the Sabbath. All Yeshua Hamashiach (Jesus, who is our shalom) was saying was that the Sabbath was made to benefit mankind. But a lot of people, especially the so-called ministers, teach their parishioners that the Sabbath was nailed to the cross, and anyone who knows Christ, knows that He didn't nail anything to the cross. What was nailed to the cross was our evil and wickedness so that we could receive redemption.

It's time for us as human beings on this planet to start speaking the truth to ourselves, and Yeshua to forgive us for our evil rebellion and greed, and start celebrating the Sabbath as there is much blessing to be gained. The blessings are in the act, just as tithing and other benevolent expressions we do as humans. We do not do these acts to get something from the Creator, who in His boundless abundance is always willing to give us the benefit of blessing because we obey Him out of love. If we only know the blessing that salvation gives, that the observance of the Sabbath gives, we would never ever stay away. This thought of the Black Sabbath is just because I personally see the blessing and beauty that I have received, and whenever I enjoy something, I like to share.

Inspiration teaches us that no one can actually get into the kingdom of the Eternal of heaven without keeping the Sabbath. I hope no one is going to run away now and say that it is the Sabbath that can save us, as only Yeshua Jesus can save us. Because we love the Lord, we obey the Sabbath, because we obey the Lord of the Sabbath. It is said, and is written and remains written, that when the consummation of all things comes to an end (which we call the judgment), and everyone gets their reward for their own works on this planet (good or bad), we will be taking a real space flight for the first time to Sion (Zion). Some people call this "going to heaven," or the great rapture.

This space flight (or whatever frame of reference you have towards that matter) that we know is where we will all take a flight on that "getting up morning" (this is going to happen whether you believe it or not). To get into the celestial realm is the greatest flight of them all; it will take seven days, and you might ask where I got that. Note that there are many things you don't know or haven't read yet. Why seven days? As you know, seven days is a perfect number, and the Eternal makes use of certain numbers.

As you can recall, the thief on the cross did not have a baptism, but Yeshua had one in the river Jordan, and this sufficed for that thief. So there are many people who didn't keep the Sabbath for various reasons (may not have known about the scriptures), so the perfect One, Yeshua, went into the synagogue on the Sabbath (as it is written and remains written) so that whoever didn't keep the Sabbath (for whatever reason) would be allotted the seventh-day flight. For those who didn't keep the Sabbath, the seventh day is allotted so that those people will get the privilege and opportunity to have a Sabbath before they have entry into their celestial home.

Remember, Isiah wrote in his book that in the new redemption of all ages, flesh, tribe, nation and people will march up to Zion to worship the Lord, from one Sabbath to the next, throughout the ages. Now we inhabit timelessness.

## The Nubian Story, African Story, Our Story, the Black Man's Story

*For the record, the expression "first black president" is not only derogatory but also racist.*

If you are a frequent viewer of CNN or CBC or BBC, or of any other mass media, you will always hear the expression "the first black president," ever since Barack Obama won the presidency of the 49th election in the USA. Let's talk about the expression, "the first black president"—or first black host, black senator or anything—what does the expression really mean? The real question must be, why didn't we have any Nubian Moorish people in those positions of power before? As a civil society of people, we have to discuss this issue in its correct context and stop gossiping when it comes to discussing matters of importance.

First, I would like to propose to the readers that the expression and the concept of "black person/people" is an incorrect one, and therefore the expression "first black president" is incorrect. Why? Because in genetic terms, you cannot define a person or human by their pigment/colour. A person is defined by their name, not their colour.

The correct way to refer to Barack Obama under the constitution in the 1800s, as the first Nubian Moor president, was that a Nubian Moor was the first president under the confederation.

Anytime the expression, the first title, is evoked, it is important to know what period of time is being spoken of, lest the statement be misleading. It is important to know that in the 1700s, the first president of what is known as the USA today, was a Nubian Moor; that is, the person you call black today. The expression "black or white people" is a new expression (white) that was coined in what is called America, to separate and divide and conquer Afro-Americans. It is also a new expression. As a matter of fact, this expression is much older than America. It is more global. It is racism. What that is all about is to tie the greatest people on Earth to a piece of property. I have been emphasizing that you cannot define a human being by their colour or land. A person is defined by their character.

We, the Nubian Moorish people, have always had our own system of worship or culture, from our own frame of reference. One of our principles is that we do not take our name from the land; we give the land its name. We are the Moorish people, who you wrongfully call black, and anyone who studies genetics knows that you cannot define human beings by their colour or pigmentation. The people you call black, our proper name is Nubian Moorish people, and we were the first to walk on planet Earth, and the first to study physics, chemistry, law and mathematics. Furthermore, we are and were the gods (we are not talking about divinity) of medicine, like Imhotep, the first physician. We are like Hannibal, the greatest of the greatest of all time in warfare, and the first to cross the Alps with his forty elephants and over twenty thousand well trained soldiers.

I was not the one who started talking about the first black this or that, but now that we are on the subject, let us really talk about the first Nubian Moorish people, the ones they wrongly call black people, and who are and were the first to stand erect on the planet. We were the ones in Eden, in the land of the gods. Always remember that whenever we use the word "god," we are not talking about divinity. The Eternal is not nameable. Whatever name we humans use to extol or exalt the most high and lofty One, they are all holy, because we use them to worship Him. But it doesn't necessarily mean that they are the Eternal's name. The Eternal reserves the right to make His name, His real name, known at his choosing, and we humans do not have to bother ourselves about that at the moment.

## Did You Know? – The Beauty of Not Knowing

Did you know—and why didn't you know—that you will never hear CNN, CBC or BBC use the expression "first white president" or the "first astronaut," or the first anything for that matter. This is because all these mediums have one thing in common. They all want to keep the false concept of white supremacy going, but you will always hear the mass media talking about the first black this or the first black that; like the first black president and first black vice president. But what does this imply? The real question should be, why doesn't the mass media highlight and tell the truth to the people about who was really the first? Like how the first man to walk this Earth was a black Nubian from Eden, North Africa; and the first who studied physics, chemistry, mathematics and law were Nubians. Do not let just anyone tell you these things; go and do your research.

Whenever the subject of the first black president comes up, one of the first things you have to ask yourself (you notice I didn't say to ask the social experts, because they are a part of the problem) is what time period they are talking about, whenever anybody says the first black this or that. Now that we are on the subject of the first black, let's talk about it in factual terms. I have been using the term "black" so far, as it is easier to understand. The correct way to define a human is not by their colour but by their real name. The real name for the people you call black, are the Nubian Moorish people.

*Obama is a special type of politician. First, he is a Nubian Moor, which makes him very humane. He also has a high degree of perception and intelligence; and in his book, he stated that he sees himself in everyone, and justice and compassion are a part of his nature.*

# Ending Racism in Our World – One way Is to stop Referring to People as White

***One of the first things we have to do (in ending racism) as individuals and a community, is to cease and desist from using the phrase "white people," because there are no white people.***

Racism is a huge problem in our world, and even though it has been a problem for years, there is an antidote to end it once and for all. I am not speaking as a naive individual but as someone who is very much aware that this is a complex matter. The Eternal (God) made us very ordinary and yet profound, but we make things and ourselves complicated. All complex matters have to have different approaches to resolve them, and we always have to look at these issues from a cause and effect perspective.

For starters, one of the first things we have to do as individuals and a community is to cease and desist from using the phrase "white people," because there are no white people, and we don't eat them. The concept or expression "white people" is a new phenomenon to our vocabulary, which was established less than a millennium ago. Actually, it is we, the Nubian, who are wrongfully called "black people," when in essence we are the gods of the planet (not divine). Over all of Europe, they were the first to be called European or white people. The expression "white people" is a construct and only means a group of people who classify themselves as privileged. Therefore, it is critical that we understand this frame of reference and that there is no human being that is white, or can be, because in genetic terms, whiteness deflects light, and light brings heat.

Just think for a moment about this as whiteness cannot absorb heat, especially when there is little or no melanin. When someone refers to themselves as "white," they are claiming that they are more privileged. Anytime they conceive that (privileged status) in their minds, the possibility exists that they will feel that they are better than others or more important. In ending racism, one of the best ways to do so is to end the idea that there are white people, or get out of our psyche that white people exist. The correct way to describe those with paler skin or less melanin is to refer to them as Caucasian, which is a branch of mankind. Racism, which is a possession or "bedevilment" of the mind (psyche), also can be eradicated if we put our will to it as it is practiced. We should not depend on the government to banish racism, as it keeps them in power. The only time it will subside is when we the people can decide how to put an end to racism and bigotry. GLORY!!! THIS IS A CALL TO CONSCIENCE.

Have you ever thought about or tried to quantify the suffering that racism causes humanity, particularly the Nubian that are wrongfully referred to as black? Why I say "wrongfully called black" is because it is foolish to define a human being because of his colour or pigmentation. I do understand why people use the words "black people." However, an intellectual person, who understands genetics and studies things from an anthropological perspective, already knows we cannot define human beings by their colour.

The fact is, black is not really a colour, even though people might refer to it as such. Furthermore, all four spectrums of colour melt into blackness to produce all the colours we see in our three dimensional world. This is why, when you go to purchase paint to paint your house, the attendant in the paint shop asks the customer to select the shade (colour) they want. The attendant then pours some tar-like substances together in a receptacle, shaking it intensely to achieve the desired shade/colour. That tar-like blackness is what gives the paint the desired colour, so the idea of something being wrong with blackness is insane and demonstrates ignorance in its highest degree.

Blackness or darkness is one of the supreme divine orders of the universe. In other words, blackness is one of the constitutions of the universe. In addition, blackness is a supreme state in which the Eternal dwelled before he created light, because ***it is the forces of darkness that produce the light.*** No one can live without darkness or blackness. Furthermore, we are all introduced to this planet Earth while in darkness, swimming around in our mother's womb, in darkness and water, so no one should use the word "blackness" in a derogatory way, because it is the divine order of authority.

Whenever one is contemplating an important subject matter, one should employ, muster or discipline their mind (spirit) to dig deep into the root/source of the subject matter. When we say "spirit," we are not talking about oxygen or breath but the spirit in man. For those of us who believe in God, let us remember that we were formed from the dust of the Earth, and for those of us who know what Earth looks like, there should be no confusion about what the shade of our skin was during creation. With that said, we were not designed for competition to be held among us, and to fight to claim who should be more privileged than the other. We are expected to work together and to do the will of God as a people in preparation for the kingdom of heaven.

**No one can quantify the suffering caused by racism.**

## Can a Human Pardon Him or Herself? Only the Sovereign Righteous One Has the Right to Pardon Himself, and He Has No Need Whatsoever

Can a justice, judge or the President, or any president for that matter, pardon him or herself? This is the subject matter that has been discussed in the United States of America and all over the world at the moment, by jurors, constitutional lawyers, judges and all legal minds. Can a judge pardon himself? It is very important for the readers to apprehend what is discussed concerning this matter. Once you can invoke the word "pardon," you are dealing with law or order. Once you have law, and you will always have law, the laws always have potential for violation. Remember that your Creator and mine uses law and mathematics to govern and rule His creation in the multi-universe.

The laws were made to maintain order, harmony and peace in the universe. That is to say that the laws were made to benefit mankind. The Eternal, the only sovereign in the entire multi-universe that dwells in the third and seventh heaven—although He cannot be contained in time or space, and who has no need whatsoever—created His law as a transcript of his character. He himself lives by His own law although He has no lack whatsoever. Humanly speaking, the Eternal is the only one who is qualified to self-pardon, although this concept of pardon does not apply to our Creator. He cannot err. Humans, on the other hand, need to humble themselves, pray and ask the most righteous One to forgive, and He will forgive and stop the madness of self-pardon, whether it be Donald Trump or anyone else.

Let us go back to where we started. We learned that the law was created for our good. We also learned that the eternal God obeys His own law, not that he has any lack. But for example, for all His creation, we also learn that there are different types of law. Let us inject for a moment that man cannot make laws. Yes, they can make rules and regulations; and in many cases, these rules and regulations are good for the community, like the Traffic Act, Immigration Act, etc.

There are numerous acts or laws that the government has on the books, some of which are unjust laws, but in many cases, these acts or laws are good for the citizens to keep the peace and harmony. Only the Creator, the eternal God, and nature can make real laws, like the moral laws of the Ten Commandments, which are eternal like the Creator himself, as we learned before. The moral law is a part of Yahweh God's character, which is immutable and cannot change and will not change.

There are a great many people who will argue their opinion, such as the government, capitalist countries and even some so-called ministers who call themselves pastors and bishops (As my sister would say, "Some were called and some just come."), who tell the people that the law of the Ten Commandments often can be nailed to the cross and are done away with. Their claim is that we are no longer under law but under grace. If truth be told, and this is not about one's opinion, we are not dealing with opinion now but dealing with the truth. Please remember that truth doesn't have contrast or opposites, just like darkness. The law and darkness are there to create balance.

The argument about something being nailed to the cross, for sure is not the moral Ten Commandments. What was nailed to the cross, remember, were the ceremonial laws of offering lambs and doves. Our dear Saviour's sacrifice of self, took care of that ceremonial law. This is what you call a lie, but it is all called spiritual treason, and anyone that continues to teach lies like this to the people, are impostors. The truth is that yes, there were ceremonial laws like killing doves and lambs. Remember that the wages one gets, for continued rebellion against the eternal law, is death. So the Lord most graciously made a temporary provision for ancient Israel to use a dove by killing that innocent bird. It was to remind them of when Yeshua Jesus will come to take their transgression or sins to the cross, for the remission of sin, and for forgiveness. That law of common no longer applies, but the law of the moral Ten Commandments is eternal, like God himself.

If truth be told, people and these so-called pastors, bishops and ministers like to tell themselves and others that the laws of the Ten Commandments are nailed to the cross or done away with. If they could speak the truth to themselves, these people would have to say that what they really want is to get rid of the Ten Commandments of the law, and the Sabbath. That is the one commandment that the so-called pastors, bishops and people want to get rid of. They are deceiving themselves and others. Remember, the eternal law of the Ten Commandments is for our good, and it is right and just. The Lord governs His vast multi-universe; thus, His laws, like the law of gravity and the law of health—and all the laws of our Creator—are designed for the good of humanity and to maintain peace and harmony. So please stop the insanity, madness and stupidity of thinking that the law of the moral Ten Commandments has been done away with.

Heaven and Earth will not pass. We will have a renewed system of things. Yes, the cosmos, and the system of man, with all of our rebellion as mankind for the past 6 to 10 millennium thousands of years, is ending or coming to an end. The new order or the rule of our loving Creator, Father Abba the most gracious, whether or not we believe it, will happen because these momentous events do not depend on us. Our sovereign Creator God will bring these things to pass, so we do not have to worry ourselves.

*One thing we do know is that all of us humans are all standing in need of prayer and pardon, forgiveness and grace and glory. May heaven help us all.*

All human beings are born with inherent rights, life, liberty and freedom, period. Another important right we have is self-defence. It is time that a person can judicate for themselves, notwithstanding that there is always the possibility for a person to act biased on behalf of oneself. That is the human nature of things we all have. To err is in our nature as humans, and this is why the discussion around the subject matter of self-pardon is very important for many people, and this is why I am sharing my frame of reference with you, the reader; so this is not an opinion.

I do not have an opinion. I discuss any subject matter based on the nature of that thing. Laws govern everything in the universe. Why does a judge or the past president—or any president for that matter—have to be flawless to pardon themselves? To pardon oneself, one has to be void of bias, which no human can be, humanly speaking—the only one who can pardon himself is Elohim, our Creator, as you know already. Yahweh God has no lack whatsoever. The Eternal has no need to pardon himself. He obeys all His laws himself, and in regard to anyone who needs to be pardoned, it simply means that they have transgressed the law of the sovereign one.

We all, as humans, need to be pardoned by the most gracious holy, His glory. I am sure that the idea of the very concept of men pardoning other men, comes from the greatest need of this planet Earth. It is for us to start loving each other and forgiving each other. That much we can do now, and start healing the world. Imagine that type of world. Heaven help us all.

*Bear in mind that the argument against self-pardon is that it is a judiciary matter. The president, etc. are executive officers. Constitutionally, it is not their place to act as judges.*

## The Duty of Memory

The entire theme of this book, or thread that binds this book together, is all about the divine order, law and mathematics. The theme and purpose of this book is to gently remind the readers about the all-important principle of the divine law, order and mathematics, which are the foundation of the governance of our Creator. Like the holy book, the entire theme of that library we call the Bible is about one person, the Christ, Yeshua Hamashiach, and His redemption for all of humanity. The reason for that is the immutable law that governs the throne of our Creator. Violation of these laws cost the Creator His life. How is that a simple thing? Could anyone, a group or individual, think that the very government of the Eternal could be slighted, negated or done away with? How can anyone infer such a thing?

So our brother, the honourable Robert Nesta Marley, was pleading with mankind with such anguish to accept the principle of humanity, to accept the government of our Creator, which are His laws, the law of the Ten Commandments, and all His laws that govern His universe. All our ancient ancestors pleaded with ancient Israel to accept the government of our Creator, which are His laws. Ancients, like Jeremiah, all entreated the people to accept the government of the Creator. All modern societies, including Canada, whether a parliamentary or autocratic system, are all governed by laws and rules and regulations. Two of these regulations come to mind: the Constitution (Apex Law) and the Charter of Rights. We have many acts that govern society, like the Landlord and Tenancy Act, and Highway and Traffic Act. If human societies have all these laws to govern the country, what about the Creator? We are repeating this theme for a reason, about the importance of the Creator. Just as the building blocks of our bodies are cells, the building blocks of our Creator are His laws.

## Written or Unwritten Laws – Which Are More Important?

There are written and unwritten laws. Which are more important? As we have discussed before, and we are saying it again, laws, whether by our Creator or human government, permeate our lives with those principles to foster order. Through this little dialogue that we have been having, we have unequivocally agreed that our Creator rules and governs His multi-universe through His laws of principles. And all these principles are for our good as humans. So let us understand, for once and forever, that our Creator—a kind, loving, merciful Creator—has no need. Therefore, everything He instructs us to do through His law and order, is for our good, our pleasure and our happiness. Once we apprehend (understand) this truth, then we will take delight in obeying these principles from an attitude of love.

Written or unwritten laws are all important and reinforce each other. So you have the written laws, like those written on tablets of stone by the Creator himself, and you have unwritten laws, like the law of gravity, law of chemistry and the law of physics. These are all living laws that if we violate them, there are consequences. So before we go on to laws that have to deal with human society, we just want to back up a little. Some of the principles we have are like the principle of love. There are laws that govern the principle of love, and let us remember that the word we call "love" is not love; it is a principle that is governed by laws—law of loyalty, honour, commitment and work. Love, itself, is based on chemistry. Chemistry is governed by law. What we call "love" is solely based on principle, and all the different types of love, like agape, parental and filial love, have the properties that constitute those principles in chemistry. You know, to have attraction, you have to have chemistry and physics. These are laws.

What about the law that governs the home? Every home is governed by law and order. Many times, as parents, we tell our children that they are out of order when they are disrespectful. When we say they are out of order, we are implying that the home is run by law and order. So, we are saying to the child that they have to keep the law of the home in order to have happiness and harmony. At the beginning of the book, we stated that there is a line of divine order in every facet of God's creation. That is why we are making reference to the home, which is the first society. There are many aspects to one's home. What about the law of the kitchen? Everyone knows that if their kitchen is not in order, they cannot do anything; meaning that it is difficult to prepare a meal. What about the bathroom law? We might say that it is not necessary to discuss this, but it is very essential, and you will find out sooner or later how important these aspects of our lives are, to maintain the order as our Creator intended.

Actually, it is said by inspiration that if our homes are not in proper order and clean, even the angelic beings will not take pleasure in visiting our homes. So you see that every facet of our lives is governed by law and order, and is for our pleasure, peace of mind and happiness. Our Creator is interested in every aspect of our lives. Through His mercy and love, He wants us to have peace of mind as His crowning act of His creation of humans.

## Human Society (Written and Unwritten Laws)

Do we need law and order in human society? Do you have written and unwritten laws in your society? Yes, for sure, we do have them in our written laws in the sense of statutes. We are still on the theme of law and order. We have laws that are inscribed into statutes that are written by parliamentarians and judges, and there are many other acts, which we mentioned previously, such as a law of the environment. A law of the environment is to stop littering or contaminating the surroundings.

What about labour laws? It is one of the oldest laws. The desire and greed for free labour by transnational corporations and businesses is why we have slavery. Because of their disregard for the law that governs labour, we still have free labour in countries such as India and Bangladesh. We will never forget how this concept of free labour resulted in over 200 million of our people dying in slavery or being disposed of at sea and otherwise.

What about the law of discrimination? These laws are written down, but there are some that are not documented or written down, like respect for our neighbours' property, land or things. Even in human law in our society, some of the content is taken from the Creator's law of the Ten Commandments, like "thou shalt not kill." These are principles from moral laws that even in human society have been cited. How can anyone even think and infer that these principles are not applicable today, in this minute, this moment and this day.

What we really need is a real awakening of consciousness to the importance of accepting and governing our lives according to the principles of, first, the laws of our Creator, and to those laws in society that are meant for the good of society and the people. Unlike our Creator's laws that are good for us, human laws, a lot of times, mean ill for society. Human laws mean ill when they follow an unjust path; and we conclude that there are many laws that are good for us as citizens, and which help to create balance and harmony. So we need to recommit ourselves as "hueman" as we discover the importance of law and order in every facet of our lives. Even if you do not agree or adhere to these principles, through one's ego and selfishness, it is important to agree with the principle of these laws, whether our Creator's laws, written or unwritten, or to acknowledge the laws that human society has created. And I know if we do, we will have a more abundant and peaceful life. May heaven help us all.

## When the Eternal (God) Refuses to Have Anyone Speak for Him on Certain Occasions. He stated: Remember, Remember, Remember

There are many times when the Eternal (God), most merciful Lord, asks humans to speak, or gives them the privilege to speak on His behalf, and there are times when the Lord stands up and speaks for himself. Whenever He does that, like a good parent, He means business (humanly speaking). The Lord, the "I Am," speaks of himself in this way on more than one occasion. The "I Am" is one of the Eternal's names, and it means "always exists and always present." When God says "I am," He is in essence appealing to our higher consciousness. If you recall, He spoke to Moses to go and speak to Pharaoh about letting His people go. Moses asked God, "Who should I say sent me?" God replied by saying, "I Am that I Am." On different occasions, the Eternal (God) also said:

- *I am the Eternal; I change not.*
- *I am the Eternal; I cannot lie.*
- *I am the God of order, not confusion (chaos and disorder).*

The Eternal is aware of our weak memory muscle, and this is why He has mercy on us; because He remembers that we are dust (earthly) and that our memory is weak. Because He knows of our shortcomings in that area, He always reminds us of important things and tells us to remember these themes:

- *Remember thy Creator in the days of your youth.*
- *Remember Lot's wife.*
- *Remember the Sabbath day to keep it holy.*

The expressions "I am" and "remember," by our Creator, are invoking His highest authority and, in this expression, the Creator is unequivocally expressing His highest ego. Ego, in this case, should not be taken or seen in a negative light, as here it means having absolute authority and doesn't need counselling from anyone or anything. All of us will do well to listen when the Creator speaks, in particular when He invokes the expression, "I am" and "remember."

The Lord says of himself, and it remains stated in the holy volume, that it is a terrible thing to fall in the hands of the Lord. In another place in the holy volume, the Eternal stated, and it remains stated, that the spirit of the Lord will not always strive with mankind. Therefore, if we fall, we should fall on the rock and be broken, and claim our redemption for which we were born or born for. Heaven help us all.

# Turn off Time, the Earth Stops Spinning. Do You Realize we Are Living on Borrowed Time?

The Eternal, our Creator, does not exist in time. He is beyond time, beyond our prayers, beyond our songs. We exist in time as humans, and He created an amount of time in which He will bring everything to conclusion. I was listening to a friend recently, who stated that from when she was a child—and now she is over 60 years old—her parents used to tell her that time is running out and the end of the world, and Yeshua (Jesus), will be coming. So the concept of time is a complex one. In our consciousness as humans, it may appear to us that time is moving slowly.

We have to remember that with our Creator, time measurement is different from humans. Our Creator stated that 1000 years or a millennium is just like a day, but as sure as the sun is shining (even if we don't see it shining, it still is shining), we are definitely running out of time, or we are living on borrowed time. The density of injustice is what is heralding the consummation of things on this planet. The determination of those who are against God's law and order is so great, and their higher power is so formidable, that they could stop the globe from spinning if the gates of freedom are not opened up widely.

3 John 2: Wealth, Health and Beauty Are Your Right

***Beloved, I wish above all things that thou mayest prosper and be in health, even as thy soul prospereth.***

# APPENDIX I

The foundation of the Uniform Commercial Code (U.C.C.) is commercial law. The foundation of commercial law is based upon certain universal, eternally just, valid, moral precepts and truths. The basis of commercial law is the Law of Exodus (i.e. the Ten Commandments) of the Old Testament and Judaic (Mosaic) Orthodox Hebrew commercial law. The laws of commerce have remained unchanged for at least six thousand years, and form the basis of Western civilization, if not all nations. This law of commerce therefore applies universally throughout the world. Real commercial law is non-judicial and is prior and superior to the basis of, and cannot be set aside or overruled by, the statutes of any government, legislature, governmental or quasi-governmental agencies, courts, judges and law enforcement agencies, which are under an inherent obligation to uphold said commercial law.

Commercial law is a "war of truth," expressed in the form of an intellectual weapon called an "affidavit." An affidavit is merely a written list of facts or truths signed under penalty of perjury and usually notarized. The person composing and signing an affidavit is called the "affiant." It is "survival of the fittest," where the last unrebutted stands triumphant. In the laws of commerce, the eternal and unchanging principles of the law are:

**1.** <u>A workman is worthy of his hire.</u> Authorities: Exodus 20:15; Lev. 19:13; Matt. 10:10; Luke 10:7; II Tim. 2:6. Legal maxim: "It is against equity for free men not to have the free disposal of their own property.

**2.** All are equal under the law (God's Law – Moral and Natural Law). Authorities: Exodus 21:23-25; Lev. 24:17-21; Deut. 1:17, 19:21; Matt. 22:36–40; Luke 10:17; Col. 3:25. Legal maxims: "No one is above the law." "Commerce, by the law of nations, ought to be common, and not to be converted into a monopoly and the private gain of a few."

**3.** In commerce, truth is sovereign. See Exodus 20:16; Psalm 117:2; John 8:32; II Cor. 13:8. Legal maxim: "To lie is to go against the mind." Oriental proverb: "Of all that is good, sublimity is supreme."

**4.** Truth is expressed in the form of an affidavit. See Lev. 5:4-5; Lev. 6:3–5; Lev. 19:11–13; Num. 30:2; Matt. 5:33; James 5:12.

**5.** A matter must be expressed to be resolved. See Heb. 4:16; Phil. 4:5; Eph. 6:19–21. Legal maxim: "He who fails to assert His rights has none."

**6.** An unrebutted affidavit stands as truth in commerce. See 1 Pet. 1:25; Heb. 6:13–15. Legal maxim: "He who does not deny, admits."

**7.** An unrebutted affidavit becomes a judgment in commerce. See Heb. 6:16–17. Any proceeding in court, tribunal or arbitration forum consists of a contest, or "duel," of commercial affidavits, wherein the points remaining unrebutted in the end, stand as the truth and the matters to which the judgment of the law is applied.

**8.** He who leaves the field of battle first (does not respond to affidavit), loses by default. See Book of Job; Matt 10:22. Legal maxim: "He who does not repel a wrong when he can, occasions it."

**9.** Sacrifice is the measure of credibility. One who is not damaged, put at risk or is willing to swear an oath on His commercial liability for the truth of His statements and legitimacy of His actions, has no basis to assert claims or charges, and forfeits all credibility and right to claim authority. See Acts 7, life/death of Stephen. Legal maxim: "He who bears the burden ought also to derive the benefit."

**10.** A lien or claim, under commercial law, can only be satisfied by one of the following actions. See Gen. 2–3; Matt 4; Revelation. Legal maxim: "If the plaintiff does not prove His case, the defendant is absolved." 10.1. A rebuttal Affidavit of Truth, supported by evidence, point-by-point. 10.2. Payment. 10.3. Agreement. 10.4. Resolution by a jury according to the rules of common law. Because truth is sovereign in commerce, and everyone is responsible for propagating the truth in all speaking, writing and acting, all commercial processes function via affidavit, certified and sworn on each affiant's commercial liability as "true, correct and complete," attesting under oath re the validity, relevance and veracity of all matters stated, and likewise demanded. Usually in written matters, such as on an IRS Form 1040, 8300, etc., voter registration application, driver's license application, notary form for document certification, application for a Treasury Direct Account, and on nearly every document that those who run the system desire anyone to sign in a commercially binding matter, signature is required under penalty of perjury, "true, correct and complete." In a court setting, however, testimony (oral commercial affidavit) is stated in the judicial equivalent by being sworn to be "the truth, the whole truth and nothing but the truth, so help me God." As well, the need for asserting all matters under solemn oath of personal, commercial, financial and legal liability, for the validity of each and every statement, participant must provide material evidence, i.e. ledgering/bookkeeping, substantiating that each fact or entry is true, valid, relevant and verifiable. Without said acceptance of liability and facts provided to support one's assertions, no credibility is established.

# APPENDIX II

## *Towards Identity and Power*
## *Were we slaves, were we captives?*

Identity and power are dialectically intertwined in ways so deep and complex, it belies the first impressions. At the heart of any undertaking of power, its use, its ensuance, its blockage, its metamorphosis and links, and at the kernel of it, lies the question of power for who and against whom. The character, be it individual, group, empire or race, who have or lack, the wherewithal of power is all the heart of such a concept. Power does not fly around the universe in the air like pollution. In human terms, it must have a source, a course and destiny. These qualifications or requisites, if I may say so, are tied to the hands of the wielder of the power. Hence, the paramount importance of identity in any discussion of power.

Where there is power, there is an identity. Yet the cognition of the identity is another can of beans. People, individuals, as well as collectives, persons or societies, could and have been proven historically to evolve, from the misty aberrations of being objects of history, to that of being conscious, subjective, aware actors on the stage of history. Both instances bear witness to the presence of power, but in the first instance, the power is not understood and consciously organized and wielded. Hence, the search for identity is, in more ways than one, the search for power with the identification of the subjects of that power. Even in all religions, the deities' powers rest on a cultural identifiable base, be it race or language or response to a calling, from where it springs to all its otherworldly claims and universalities. Its messages, which are more imperative than the other, are obviously nugatory questions, as none can exist or flourish without the other.

The lack of power is impotence, and the grip that it has on black people, and the world over historically, though not always as well as the precarious present to which we are living witnesses, is but the history of our collective endeavours in the last struggling centuries of the destruction of our civilization. The primary attack or the onslaught on the black civilization has been and continues to be the denial of a people of their identity. That outright obliteration of identity, and the miasma of confusion that accompanies it, renders the people as lost sheep, unaware of the power they wield, and they are so ignorant and demeaned that some accept as their natural lot in life to be servile, to be domesticated and to be decided for fear, power and independent practice of it, as our merchants are afraid of the importation of factories and machines, and our intellectual panic before the production of new ideas.

The hand that is afraid to wield power is a hand that does not know to whom it belongs. When one knows who he/she is, they know where their power comes from, and where its destination is. We need not go back on the litany of admonitions and advices of our heroic thinkers regarding the peril of ignorance of one's history. For without history, there is no identity, and with a lack of history, there is a lack of self-expressing one's identity; and without identity, the people are reduced to a nation of sheep pasturing by the slaughterhouse. It is a testament to power, and a miracle that many of our brothers and sisters spoke to us from within the slaughterhouse.

From Pushkin to Spartacus, from Wole Soxinkh to the oral griots of pastoral Africa, from Malcolm X to Oliver Thambo, from Harriet Tubman to Angela Davis, from Billie Holiday to Mariam Makeba and Halima Khalif Magool—an endless corridor of candles that lit the way to liberation, as much as they could, while struggling in the belly of the beast; and nothing is more beastly than the denial of the people's identity. Now then, the chronicle of the history of a people, their collective memory, is the endeavour and struggle to elevate the people from a population to the nation, to paraphrase the great Senegalese scholar, Cheikh Anta Diop, who said that a people without historical memory is not a nation but a population.

A source of pernicious power of destructive and divisiveness lies in the definition of a people by others rather than the self. The trajectory of loss and oppression is self-evident in the parroting of the definition of others to one's self. All that brings me to the point of departure. My concern here in this vast area of study and life is to illustrate that the language that people use, the labels they carry, the heritage they hail from and progression towards destiny of freedom and liberation, is of vital importance in the nexus of identity and power. One need not look too far to realize that power without identity is impotence, and identity without power is zombieism.

A point at hand is the way the history of the capture and the exploitation of our people, known generally as slavery, could be misleading and disempowering construct. The stigma of slaves, slavery, the slave trade, etc., carries within it the a priori that these were slaves waiting for a master, and with its arrival, commenced the slave trade. But the historical facts fly in the face of this, and I hope more serious and seminal work is done in this area. The business of enslaving people is an inappropriate labelling of a people who were captured in wars and transported to an opposite land, and predatorily exploited for centuries. It was not the case of societal devolution to pauperism and servitude; it was rather the product of an instrument of war and captivation. In that regard, the labelling of the captives as slaves, and the process of slavery, is an unsuitable, linguistic inferioration with an extension into the post "emancipation times," with stigma of shame, worthlessness and degraded humanity, if not the outright denial of that humanity to them.

The generations born after the fact, have fallen and continue to live in the duress of their folk having been slaves at one time, not to mention the continuation of the phenomenon after legal declarations have been issued by the predators. Consequently, it is more apt and correct to call that period in our history as "the long captivity." It is captives that aspire for freedom, for the breaking of the bonds of arrest and captivity; "slavery" is a spiritually deadening phenomenon.

Our people went through the hell and the shadows of the valley of death, not willing but as captives waiting, working and praying, and fighting for emancipation in general and for the liberation of the individual from the signs and symptoms of the yoke of captivity. So we are not the children of former slaves; we are children of the long captivity, and our march to liberty and freedom goes on as it did during the days of hunting down the people for captivity in the plantations of America and Europe. Therefore, the captivity that our people went through can be divided into three major categorizations: the long captivity in Arabia, Europe and the Americas. Secondly was the colonial period, where there was captivation in our own territories, and it could be historically labelled "short captivity." Thirdly is the ongoing insidious process of degradation, discrimination and outright exploitation of the people's minds and muscle that is au pied as we breathe now, which I tentatively call "the hidden captivity." Nothing is more paramount in battle and in people's historical marches than the morale of the people. That morale, that elation of intellect and material production, can be enhanced or dwarfed by the language and the landmarks that the people use.

The demoralization carried on of the slave title and slavery legacy is a permanent stamp on the freeborn soul of our people. The fact of the matter is that we have never been slaves as a people; we were captives, and we march on the pathways of freedom, not as former slaves or grandchildren of former slaves, or brothers of erstwhile slaves, but as former captives, grandchildren of former captives, and brothers and sisters of erstwhile captives. The narratives of slavery should be replaced by the narrative of captivity. Nothing can hold a man captive but himself, and nothing can stand between a people and their pursuit of emancipation from captivity.

**By: Salah Jama Hussein**
***Lamentation of the Sun***

# APPENDIX III

## Fraternal Preventive Diplomacy (Rwanda Genocide)

The main idea comes from the observation of a recurring pattern of conflict and bloodletting in the African continent. This has ramifications to all African descendants in the Caribbean and all over the world. The reason for this transcends the eternal bond of fraternity of the children of the African continent, be they at home or overseas.

Further than that, it has to do with common patterns of history, in both spheres, that our people have been subjected to. This includes, among a litany of other historical disruptions and dislocations, the ominous landmarks of the long or protracted captivity of our people in the Middle East, in Europe and in the Americas.

It also has to do with the ferocity and deep rooted exploitive and dehumanizing strategies of colonialism, neo-colonialism and the ramification of impartial reach that continues as of this writing in the name of globalism, and is worse than Covid masks of the new world order.

An odious dimension is the lack of democratic rule, and autocratic and parasitic governments, or lack of governance, that goes unabated under the protection of world capitalism and the tentacles of multinational corporations. In addition to the savage, material exploitation of the continent's wealth, and the zapping of its fruitful labour, it goes further and deeper into the destabilization of popular authorities, massacre of the revolutionary youth and intelligentsia, and the placement of puppets and traitors in their stade, frustrating and dwarfing popular participation and legitimate leadership. None of this is new. It has been a nauseating repetitive cycle, now here and now there.

In the past century, these schemes of control, and drainage of the brain and muscle from us, have taken genocidal proportions, such as the event for which we are here today to remember and pray over its victims. A question arises from these sordid experiences: Is it possible to work out a program of action that points researchers to possible turmoil and the weak, prone to exploitation in the areas of the bodies, politics and societies of our people, and move ahead of time, in preventive diplomatic, fraternal resolution, and awareness and consciousness-building endeavours? And if the possibility of work honestly is there, can we prevent such calamities, or at least mitigate them before they take their toll? This short note of mine is an invitation to brainstorm among the really concerned, intellectuals, clergy and statesmen, so that humanity and goodwill returns to our continent and its future.

**By: Professor Salah J. Hussein**

# APPENDIX IV

## Depression: The Social Dimension

**The most effective way to keep people (or a person) on their knees, oppress them and also claim to be looking after them, is to turn the people against themselves.**

It is very hard to define depression in a rational scientific manner that covers all of its manifestations. The reason for that is obvious. This is a disease where the source and trajectory vary from person to person, society to society, era to era. It is, by its nature, also irrational, and wide and encompassing in its grip and devastation; so much so that the phenomenon of depression is used by exploitative races and classes as a weapon that they wield against the health and the uprising of the people.

If you remember how sexuality, deviance, drugs, alcohol and other means of demoralization are used against downtrodden people, you'll see the vast impact that depression has had, and the medicating drugs that go with it and have been used, and are still being used against black people universally, and against the oppressed masses of the world. The plethora of feel-good pharmaceuticals that are in the marketplace to numb the conscience and dwarf the healing initiative of the people, is obvious to the naked eye and is a living memory in the saga of oppressed people. Freedom is an innate goal of divine order ordained in all living beings, but it had long been argued that the most effective way to keep people (or a person) on their knees, oppress them and also claim to be looking after them, is to turn the people against themselves. When the personality of a being is at war with itself, it is very farfetched to find redemption for its malady. Nobody can defeat man but himself: when the person destroys the gut of his fabric and freedom from within, with his own hands and power.

Due to this reason, among others, I consider the phenomenon of depression as an instrument of war. It is studied in elaborate scientific ways as a means of captivating people and enslaving them. The stark fact that depression is a slow meticulous killer, and that it invariably leads to suicide and other forms of death, is enough to testify to its obvious power of destruction and demise. Having said that, I am not forgetful that through the annals of human history, man has been able to find solutions to seemingly unsolvable problems, vistas to seemingly endless blockages, and routes to freedom in a seemingly endless abyss. The inventiveness of the spirit of human beings is boundless. It is even greater when that spirit is connected to the higher spirit that had endowed it with life, called God or higher power Christ or Allah. The realignment with the divine purpose of creation is a sure route to health and freedom; and depression, like other ailments, can be tackled to that endeavour. In the search for miracle drugs, they sink into self-pity and "shrink" services, and the addiction to pills or drugs to take away the pain, when they are only digging the foxhole of the disease deeper, and that is the crown of the enemy. It is a satanic disease.

On another note, we remarked that the origins of this disease and its kin family of melancholia are not easily definable. What makes it difficult to pin down to an exact address of issuance, is that it has a cultural, temporal and personal scientific nature. Hence, the variations, the variegation and also the variety of routes to tackle it and overcome it. Though the differences are a lot and numerously confusing, one thing is for sure: The spiritual healing of this disease is the correct route for the person, the society and for the times.

Now allow me to narrow down a handful of suggestions that experience—personal as well as societal—has convinced as a cure and a way forward from despair to hope, from impotence to power, from surrender to will, from death by the installment plan to a meaningful life and daily celebration of life and liberty. First and foremost, among these, is the realization that you, the individual, is not alone in this. It is happening to many people, and it has happened before, so there are others in this war who are on your side. Nothing debilitates the person more than the belief that they are lonely, forlorn victims. This group feeling gives the soul a sense of solidarity with other souls. And that is a source of power.

Alienation, the separation of people from one another, and the absence of honest, social communication among the people, is one of the key strategies of this disease. The more people talk to one another, the more they connect with one another, and the more people pray together, the more they engage in common social activities, such as services, sports, picnics, etcetera, and the more that energy of interaction elevates the spirit of the person and the group.

As of old, loneliness is the bringer of madness; it is also the promoter of disease and of despair. The reason is simple. No man is an island unto himself. We are social beings, and our health and well-being depend on the cohesiveness of the group, and on the sense of belonging of the one to all, and all to one. This is a divine arrangement. There is a point that is so important in my consideration that I would like to reiterate again—and I can't say it any stronger—that point is the power of prayer. The spiritual energy of the prayer touches the heart and fabric of each and every individual, so that prayer, as a spiritual phenomenon, liberates the body from the grip of downward swinging emotions, heals the body particle, and sets the person free from depression and drugs and misery.

**By: Dr. Salah Jama Hussein**

# APPENDIX V

## Totalitarianism of a Crowned Virus and the COVID Merchants The rich get richer and the poor die.

April 19, 2021
Professor Salah J. Hussein

In Buroa, the eastern regional capital of the struggling state of the Republic of Somaliland, the scene of mass burial earlier last month, of hundreds (at one point, three hundred fifty) of people put into mass graves, brought to our attention the ominous spectre of this cruel pandemic, COVID-19. There was no time for practicality, ritual or Kaddish, as heaps of bodies were intermed into the soil like in times of war. The gruesome image left a heartbreaking impact on people all over the world, at a time when empathy, etc. are in short supply and the whole globe is tottering with the impact of the virus. In Africa and other third-world countries, what happened in Buroa is becoming commonplace. The indiscriminate onslaught of this pandemic leaves no room for reflection, meditation or prayer. It is a biblical, gloomy reality that has to be taken by these weak, evolving, struggling societies, with the solemn numbness that we register earthquakes or, as it has been before, by imperialist holocaust.

Entire histories and people are being wiped from the face of existence as we know it, with no end in sight. Of course, there is hope. Without it, life would be a long tunnel of despair. But it might be difficult to harbour hope in circumstances of such overpowering carnage. The dream that one day diseases will no longer be with us, seems to have been receding into the realm of puerile fantasy. Yet life goes on. Others are born and are oblivious to these circumstances. History repeats itself, and hope and life, and survival, reassert themselves. And so it has been through the annals of human history.

Observation of these tragic episodes and the breakdown of struggling society at the backbone, recalled for me the Zulu lamentational saying that kingdoms wax and wane, and springs that were mighty go dry. It is needless to wallow in the valley of despair, as it serves no positive purpose. Let us conclude this trying, despairing experience, with the simple note that we should forever remember that the sun rises. Having said that, and on a lighter note, the other day, I remarked in a discussion with friends, that Covid is perhaps the curse of Karl Marks on contemporary societies. His dream of the inevitability of the coming of the communist society has met with one of the grandest failures in human history. This Covid pandemic seems to have many characteristics in common with the theory and the cruel application of communist thought in modern history. Allow me to tentatively enumerate some of those ironic similarities.

1. Just like the envisioned "dictatorship of the proletariat," Covid also incurred a heavy toll in human cost.
2. Just as in the case of victims of totalitarianism under Stalin and others, there is no recourse for justice for its victims.
3. Like communism, it (Covid that is) restricted people's mobility, inhibited and outlawed person-to-person communication, hampered the flow of information and quarantined people apart, under an apparatus called "state of emergency."
4. Covid, like communism, expropriated the public spaces for the people, and restricted individuals into monitored fox holes. The author of these lines is now in one of those respites whose end is not on the horizon.
5. Like international communism, Covid has a global sway that bounces over the borders of land and sea, tradition and culture,

religion and race. It is international in its scope, global in its sweep and blind in its destruction. In that sense, it has become a spectre that unites us; so much so that the term "humanity" is coming back to the love of ordinary, daily narrative. That is evinced in the media, ex-cathedra, etc., just as we are evoking it here in the pages of the Jamaican Xpress.

6. Like the promise of communism or fascism, the shape of the world after Covid is unknown, unpredictable and open to the verisimilitude of our hope, our struggles, our troubles and our despair.
7. It has a leveling quality. Like fascism or communism, a lifestyle of overboard equality is introduced by the dictatorship of this crowned virus, but within that egalitarian appeal and annihilation. There are latitudes of equality put in place in all societies. The north is not suffering as the south, the poor are more compounded than the rich, and the industrial societies are better than the agrarian or pastoral societies.
8. As under communism, there is an orchestrated (or naturally necessary perhaps) blending of propaganda and information. It goes further. Propaganda and knowledge are used as a substitute to one another and, invariably, propaganda is given an upper hand. Look at the loss of trust among all sorts of people of the media, press, information technology, etc., as well as the pronouncements of leaders and government. The feeling that there will be no access to true information, and that there is a hidden agenda at play, is in the minds of most people all over the world. Such was the feeling of the people under the social engineering of totalitarianism.
9. Like communism and other variants of totalitarianism, it is an epochal revolution whose destiny extends into the future with peril, hope and mystery.
10. Like totalitarianism, it is going to rise to a new nascent class—call them "Covid merchants" or "traders of disease."
11. Like totalitarianism, with all promises of "reform" or vaccination, the new spectre has the flag of fear hovering over the heads and

hearts of humanity.

12. Just like survival under totalitarian dictatorship, people resort to new techniques of coping, of overcoming and of rationalizing, along with new speech. Remember the double talk syndrome and a new double therapy phenomenon, where the prescribed procedures are considered to be their carriers of the malady. Finally, to live or not to live becomes their paramount concern of the agenda of humanity. As in Hamlet, the mantra becomes, "To be or not to be." In gripping circumstances of such a type, the formation of any civilized way of life becomes a vitally tested enterprise. Good luck, and keep the hope alive.

PS: The writers are paying a solemn tribute to the illustrious Dr. Aden Yusut Abokor, a graduate of the University of Warsaw, Poland, who died as he was medicating the victims of the Covid pandemic in Somaliland. He died a heroic, humane death in the service of others. Peace be upon his soul.

1. Professor Salah Hussien
2. Mecropolis – City of the Dead
3. The African Table Talk
4. The African Presence

# APPENDIX VI

## Safe is the city of swords as its boundaries, or of justice as its boundaries.

### Justice Is an Example

In ancient Greece, at the height of the city-state democracy, there occurred a debate. That rings in the annals of history for its timeless significance in history. In the euphoria of the might and grandeur that was Hollas, one of the senators asserted, as a politically veritable fact, that safe is the city that has its sword as its boundaries. The senator, of course, was referring to the might and defensive ability of a city to deter any onslaught of its structure, and function from above, within or from the outside.

Power gives one the assurance of peace and justice, and the deterrence of any enemy from incurring hurt or pain. But when you look closely, is that really the truth? Is it might that guarantees our safety as cities, countries or individuals? Is it our ability to respond with the sword, to fell the adversary and make our circumstances peaceful?

Logic and history unite the proof that that is not the case. In that debate, another senator, wiser and more seasoned in the affairs of state and the mood of the flow of history, rebutted the earlier senator. He said, "I beg to differ with the proposition of my friend." I believe he stated that safe is the city that has justice as its boundaries. When justice is instilled in the culture of the people, and people are protected not by the firearms that they carry but by the just legal system they live under, then we have peace, we have growth, we have liberty, and we have freedom from fear, freedom from tyranny, freedom from armed, combatant abuse of the dignity and life of the citizens.

We have to remember that justice is not an end in itself. It is a process that facilitates and enhances the movement from crime to civility. Justice is usually, and more often than not, a panacea or redress for the victims, whether mortally killed or injured, whether hurt in body or psyche. The process of justice will not bring the old status quo of things to the victimized individual. It is a pointer. It is hopefully a landmark to forestall, stop, defuse and discourage the act of aggression and the assaults on human life and morals. That is why I say that justice is really an example. And the victims of injustice provide us with a scapegoat so that others do not go through the plight that the former victims have gone through. And because of the unity of human experience and the interconnectedness of our lives, it is the best thing that we can humanly provide and fight for, short of resurrecting the destroyed past.

We cannot wipe the tears from the victim that is gone, but we can do that for the living that he/she left behind. And that is commendable, and that is the example of justice.

**By: Professor Salah Hussein**

# APPENDIX VII

## COVID-19 – Time, Reflection Season

We have shared many burning, current issues throughout this book, and have also travelled together to the past, both glorious and testing for our people. We spoke of different places, like Egypt, Ethiopia and Timbuktu. All along, we relied on the understanding and the intellectual, as well as the commercial support, of you all. It is with hope that I write to you about these COVID-19 times. It is also with faith and hope that we navigate this biblical storm of a pandemic. We have faith in our Creator to assist us as we humbly walk with Him and pray for salvation and reprieve. It is our deep hope that we, as humanity, all by and large, learn a lesson of wisdom from this harrowing experience.

Here is where love enters the centre stage of our lives—to love one another, to love the Creator, to love our Saviour, to love ourselves. On that note, we are happy to share this element of loud meditation with you. Since we are obliged to spend a lot of time at home and invariably alone, I suggest that we fill this time with calls, letters and communication with our elders that we had no time for, and with the loved ones we missed for so long.

Remember how much time our children and young needed of us, which we could not afford because of the obligations and the hustle and bustle of life. Now is the time to do all those things and, above all, this is a good time for personal growth, inner inventory and thinking of your beliefs and faith, direction and action.

To know yourself is of the essence of being, and to learn of yourself, for yourself, by yourself, opens venues of critical enlightened thinking. Doxology has no room here. We are not docile, passive objects. We are living, inquisitive, pioneering people. Finally, remember what Christ told us: "As you think, you are." So let us see this pandemic as a blessing in disguise, and think well for ourselves. With that clarity of thinking, we approach the truth, which takes us to the gate of freedom.

**By: Professor Salah Hussein**

# The Man and the Book

Covid Times;

Reflection Seasons
Or
Reflection in
The Time
Of Pandemic.

Unveiling Speech

The Man and the Book

It's worthy of early and quick note that the writer, his work, and the introduction of unveiling the book are so intertwined; That it should not take us by much surprise when we are confronted by adamant reality, of inability to address one without the other.

The inspiration of this book, a book tall of promise, and not lacking in controversy, comes to us through the voice of a pastoral preacher, yet a man of diverse worldly influences and experiences. But prior to that, perhaps the chief arching motive in the life of this promising, broad-hearted writer, is the fact that he identifies himself as a NUBIAN.

An heir of Black Culture and African Civilization; blended with that is; the historical fact that he hails from the Caribbean, from the Island of Jamaica, the heart-breaker of the Caribbean brothers and sisters.

He spent his transformative years, well-raised, well-tutored, and well-disciplined. The main actor in his life had been, and has been and remains to be his towering father, who had the qualities of a renaissance man. Benevolent, talented, bequeathed with rare gifts of insanity and creativity, with also superb leadership qualities. He was a giant among his contemporaries; and the example, and behest he imparted on his son, Maxwell is palpable to his very expressions to this day.

That role model, and expansive personality of his father made up from the vacuum he left by the early departure of his mother. He is his father's son. That had him mature very snickly, and bear responsibility at an early age. His mind was called to so many fields and pastures.

He had an interest in words, machines (), jewellery, blacksmith's-man ship, horses, books ets..... But in the crystallization of all those trends and tendencies, he came out a pastor, preacher of the word, and a caller to the route of his savior and God. He kept all the other activities subordinate to that. Hence, his mixture of business and philanthropy, counseling and publishing magazines; social work and looking after an extended family.

A bit hard-headed and a bit of pride had him in perpetual cross-purpose with the oppressive prevailing times. He is a revolutionary; he is also a patient graphalist. In his prose and speeches he echoes the sixties; when the temper of change and movement was at its zenith. Yet, in his sermons, he is off-balanced by a patient, didactic, untiring information and inspiration.

Perhaps, as an evidence of this; I may recall his avid interest in the social, psychological, and evolutionary issues of women and children. In the first, he found fascination and wonder in their self-creation, and playful development.

In the later, he saw the very destiny of mankind; as they are the source and guarantor of life itself.

Brought up mother-less, he is caught in the web of destiny wherein he is learning and teaching the harvest of motherhood, their gift to humanity, and the soul behind all these teening souls.

His life's work can be measured by grading of failure and success. In the triumph is the seed of new tasks to tackle; and in the short-comings, we say the complexity of the road less travelled that Mr. Maxwell has chosen for himself.

It seems that this man had been calling upon himself the travail of the saints.

His portion has been blissful, but difficult and taxing. He spent many murky years in the valley of self-knowledge and self-realization; and out of that saga into his understanding of the meaning of man and God, and in his soul-searching voyage into the mysteries of creation, he came out with a long meditation, and a chronicle of his truths; which is the body and flesh of this book.

There are tears and toil in this piece of work; yet there are moments of transcendence and peace.

He is earthly, and also special; particularly yet cosmic, extravagant yet printed.

The unveiling occasion of this work is an invitation to further inquiry and illumination of other aspects of the issues covered by this work.

It is also an open, whole-hearted prayer that others will supply their constructive criticism, that may make coming editions more correct to the theme and merit of the subject; Divine Order of Authority.

**THANK YOU**.

I would like at this juncture to welcome Mr. Diamond to say a few words on behalf of himself, the Jamaican Express, and The Diamond Institute.

Look at the stars; Look at the sun; Look at the moon; you see and live in daytime and night time. These glorious stars and our earth don't move apart, nor run into one another.

Each star, like each creature, has a path. Otherwise, life would not be possible for any of us. It would not have been possible for all living things; the animals, the trees, the fish, the birds.

So, just imagine the power that keeps in place that order; the design of Yhwh (God).

That power of creation and management is the Divine Authority of the Eternal.

Just as our parents and guardians are responsible for raising us, feeding us, buying us clothes and toys, taking us to school; Our creator (God) is the ultimate raiser, feeder, clothes and educator of the Universe.

Just as there is a timetable, discipline and order in the house, and in school; there also is in the big house we live in; The Universe.

There is no room here for chaos and confusion. There is no room for error. There is no room for chance.

Everything is exactly accounted for and follows an order of set rules, which brings and keeps harmony to creation and the universe at large.

Blindness to the majesty and power of the supreme is the height of stupidity. It begets bad luck. Also, those that are ignorant are in another form of blindness; Ignorance is an act of blindness and he who a walk in the world as such, is but a poor victim of what comes his way.

Thus the importance of being open-eyed; to see and deeply understand what one sees. In order to understand anything, one should ask questions and in that manner, it becomes possible to be awake, as Christ has told us.

My young readers; you have seen how happy you become when you do what your parents and teachers ask of you. Also, how happy they feel for you and with you. They are proud of you. So, I can only imagine the happiness of the supreme when we do what he ordered us to do.

Above all else; we should not take another god besides him, our creator. In addition, we should observe the Sabbath.

I know, as you know that we humans cannot know everything there is in creation. However, in addition to the knowledge we have, we have faith which makes us put our trust in our lord.

This trust can be likened to the trust of our parents, for we are his children, his handiwork, his pupils, his cheerleaders, his singers, his dancers. We depend on Him, we rely on him and by faith we trust Him.

Remember that; Faith,
Hope,
And Love.

Faith and hope last long but above all, Love is forever. Such is the love of the supreme for us; such should be our love for our father who is in heaven.

This love is of a special kind, limitless, unconditional, it has no beginning and no end. It never becomes of lesser value but in actuality, it is ever increasing, becoming more and more, it deepens and touches every corner of our lives. The love that sustains our life.

As food gives our bodies energy and power, this love also gives us energy and power. It gives us Joy, pleasure, happiness and nothing else can substitute its power.

That is, nothing else can take its place, nor do the wonders it does.

For that we give thanks, we praise the beauty and wisdom of our lord. We pray to Him and ask for help, we ask for all that we need; all that is good for us. He will also feed and shelter us, protect us. He keeps us happy and joyful.

It is our responsibility to thank our lord, give gratitude for His favor on us. So much our lord loves us, even more than the love of the mothers. That is the way He loves us, loves our mothers, our fathers, our brothers, our sisters, and all that He created.

Therefore, in conclusion let us get together, and unite our voices as we say, as we sing and think of the praise of our creator. Lets praise him in the morning, praise him in the noontime, in the evening, night time, when you need help, when happy or unhappy. He is a river of happiness, Love and Joy.

Praise Him on the hills, on the mountains, on the plains, on the bare land, on the sea.

And, may God bless you.

## Important Note

I hereby request the assistance of Ms. Mercy to simplify the language a bit, to appeal to the children and young adults.

### Footnotes to History

Remember that Semitic means group expression.

Remember: There is chronological time and astral time or (Solar).

Remember to observe the Sabbath.

Remember: You might know much about many different things, but you might not know where you are.

Remember: Tribes in South Africa preserve the rabbinical DNA of genuine Israelites.

Remember: European manufacture of Judaism is not the genuine story.

Remember, things are not always what they seem to be.

Remember: Lot's wife became a pillar of salt because she was a traitor; and salt was abundant in the Red Sea area.

Remember: 'Lovers do not meet and fall in love; they are in each other all along'. Rumi.

Remember to use your rights; hard earned rights such as voting, to elect those you trust and favor.

Remember: We had to struggle with blood and tears to have the right to vote.

Remember: By participating in the election process, you are participating in shaping the future.

Remember: We are more powerful than we perceive ourselves to be.

Remember: Knowledge and belief is power.

Remember that ignorance is impotence.

Remember: Identity is paramount; otherwise your legacy will be claimed by others.

Remember: The fear of God is the height of wisdom.

Remember: To despair is worse than to sin.

Remember: The opposite of love is not hate; it is indifference.

Remember: Silence in the face of injustice is an approval of that injustice.

Remember: The arch of life is very long but it tilts towards justice.

Remember: Friendship is a sacred promise.

Remember: Your word is your bond.

Remember to love one another as Christ loves you.

Remember: Blessed are the peacemakers for they shall be called the children of God.

Remember: Blessed are the meek in spirit, for they shall see God.

Remember: Good things happen to those who wait.

Remember: Patience is a virtue.

Remember: Nothing is more precious in the sight of God than the death of his martyrs.

Remember: God loved you before you loved him; nay; before you even knew him.

Remember: Know the truth and the truth shall set you free.

Remember to not die in bad company.

Remember: The quality of character of the friends you keep; for birds of the same feather flock together.

Remember: Every fool will find another fool to admire him. Remember to be the head of the people, not the tail.

Remember to love your brother whom you can see, than God whom you do not see.

Remember: Your brother needs your help, God needs your generation.

Remember: Attitude is a small word but goes a long way.

Remember: To speak the truth and the truth shall stand by you.

Remember: It is grace that saves us; not our calculated work.

Remember that with the help of God, nothing is impossible.

Remember to leave the world behind, carry your cross and follow Christ.

Remember: Unity is power.

Remember: The people united, can never be defeated.

Remember: Because of you, I am.

Remember: There is a time of eternal life in the blossom of God.

Remember: There is a time to love; there is a time to hate.

Remember: With repentance, you can be born all over again.

Remember to be kind to strangers for we have been, and still are strangers here.

Remember that God is the Light of the Universe.

Remember that by the light of God, we see light.

Remember to Remember.

# COME AND BEHOLD - A CALL TO CONSCIENCE

**The beginning is in the end, so the end is in the beginning. The cause is in the effect, so the effect is in the cause**

**UNITY**

**I AM**

**BECAUSE OF YOU**